Struc

The ^{unedited} first year of
"Doctor on the House"

Jeff Howell

Further copies of this book may be purchased
for £9 incl. p&p from
Nosecone Publications
P O Box 24650
London E9 7XQ

Tel: 0181-533 3046

NOSECONE PUBLICATIONS

First published 1998
Reprinted (with index) 1999

Nosecone Publications
P O Box 24650
London E9 7XQ

Tel: 0181-533 3046

Every effort has been made to ensure the accuracy of the information in this book. Neither Nosecone Publications nor the author accept liability for any loss or expense incurred as a result of relying on any particular statements made in the book.

ISBN 0 9534557 0 X

Typesetting by
DL Graphics Ltd.
64 Old Street
London EC1V 9AN

Printed by
Digital Copy Centre Ltd.
9-10 The Oval
London E2 9DT

Contents

The first Doctor on the House column appeared in The Independent on Sunday on the 16th March 1997, following a chance meeting with Richard Phillips, who was then editing the property section.

As a former bricklayer, I have always been amazed at the way the British property professions and the construction industry offer such a shoddy service to the public, and I had the idea that people might be interested in a few observations about the industry from the inside.

The many readers' letters I have received since then confirm that I was right; there is a great interest, and a great need for unbiased information about building. Too many homeowners have had the experience of being misadvised by ignorant architects and surveyors, and mis-sold products and services by salesmen who call themselves "surveyors".

Successive British governments have paid lip service to getting rid of "cowboy" builders, but none of them is ever prepared to introduce and police the registration scheme needed to do this.

I cannot claim to have offered any remedies for the state of the British building industry, but I hope my description of the way things are may have given readers the confidence to make their own informed decisions about their homes, rather than be led by incompetent professionals and unscrupulous salesmen.

The real success of the first year of the column is measured by the number of rude letters to the editor from pompous architects, dodgy damp-proofers and double glazing salesmen, complaining that I am costing them business. I take this as a sign of real achievement.

Jeff Howell, 13th October 1998

Do-It-Yourself (16/3/97)

Doing-it-yourself may seem like an obvious way of saving money on home improvements, but if you're not careful it can end up costing you more than employing professional builders. And it can make your home worth less, as well. There are several reasons for this. Trade prices for one. For example, you or I just *cannot* get carpets as cheaply as carpet fitters can. Don't ask me why. I am (still) a card carrying bricklayer, who considers it a matter of family honour to talk his way into trade discounts. But carpets are a no-go area. There is a carpet Mafia out there and they will not sell to anyone but their own. So, if you get a decent carpet fitter you will probably get the job done, materials, labour, underlay, grippers, little brass strips at the doors etc, for less than the cost of buying the stuff at B&Q. Simple. And you won't need to buy any special tools; all you have to do is put up with the fag smoke for a couple of hours.

But what about decorating, plastering, electrics? Surely there are huge labour costs to be saved here? Well, yes, maybe. You know those figures which show that nuclear power stations are net consumers of energy? Apparently, when you add it all up, constructing it, mining the uranium, processing it, reprocessing it, guarding the waste for a thousand years, disposing of the contaminated building etc, it turns out it's not worth it. Well, the same is often true of DIY. Do-it-yourself building work can become a net consumer of money and materials, and the waste products are too horrible to contemplate – divorce, heart attacks, lack of sleep, chemical poisoning, smiling at the dustmen, etc.

On the other hand, doing-it-yourself *can* be therapeutic, satisfying and save you money too. How to decide: If you can do-it-yourself and produce a professional quality job, then you've probably saved money (but see carpet fitting, above). In the case of the wet trades – plastering and bricklaying – you can enjoy yourself and save a not inconsiderable sum. But be warned, if you attempt these tasks and achieve anything less than perfection then it will be obvious for ever. It will come under the same category as disposing of nuclear waste – future generations will have to cope with your mistakes. These tasks are difficult; even professionals lose their touch if they don't do the job every day.

But some DIYers are determined to do everything themselves, and if they can't do plastering they will seek an alternative, such as covering things up with hardboard. Hardboard figures large in the life of the DIYer. Go into any builders' merchants on a Saturday morning and you will see men in cord trousers buying hardboard. They are not buying it for its intended purpose, which is lining floors; they are buying it because they think they cannot do plastering. They are using it to cover airing cupboards and ceilings, which they will attempt to disguise with wood chip wallpaper and emulsion paint. And nobody will be fooled, and their homes will be worth less than before they started.

But back to carpets. My neighbour recently fell for the cheap carpet scam; you know, the one where the guy knocks on the door and says he's just finished fitting some carpets up the road and, guess what, he's got enough left to do your front room for £20. Well, the neighbour went for this, and decided to save even more money by fitting the carpet himself. But that's another story.

Bricks and Mortar (23/3/97)

So my neighbour bought this carpet from a bloke at the door. Now, you know you should never, ever, buy things at the door. We all know that. But, faced with this unbelievable bargain of enough brand new carpet to do the front room for £20, the neighbour's greed overcame him. So he tried to fit it himself with nails – some inch-and-a-half round heads he had in the shed. He put one through a pipe and the leak brought the ceiling down in the basement kitchen below. It cost him £165 for an emergency plumber and £90 for a plasterer, and about £60 for take-aways while the kitchen was out of use. Oh, and there wasn't quite enough carpet either.

So there's a good example of how DIY can be a net consumer of money. And there are plenty of other stories like that. Some of the worst mistakes occur because people are scared to ask for advice; they don't like to admit they don't know.

Bricklaying is a good example of this. Bricklaying mortar is made by mixing sand and cement and water, right? Wrong. Bricklaying mortar is made by mixing sand, cement, hydrated lime, plasticiser and water. The lime makes the mortar more 'fatty' and easier to handle. The plasticiser makes it flow without having to add too much water. If you just use sand and cement it won't flow unless you make it really wet, and then the mortar dribbles out of the joints and down the face of the brickwork, giving a characteristic DIY appearance.

But people don't ask. They get the idea that they want sand and cement, probably from their dads, who were accountants or bus drivers or something, and so they walk into the builders' merchants on Saturday morning and ask for sand and cement. And everyone in the builders' merchants knows what's going on but nobody says anything. They just think what a plonker. And then they watch while chummy strains himself trying to put the bag of cement into the car holding it at arm's length, away from his clean jumper. Don't ever try this, by the way; it gives you a permanent lower back injury; hug that bag tight to your chest, and follow it into the car. You can hoover the car out and you can wash your jumper but you can never fix your back.

Anyway, instead of asking for sand and cement, you should go up to the counter and say excuse me, I'm a complete plonker, please tell me what I need to make bricklaying mortar. Everyone in the place will immediately become your friend. The staff and other customers will vie with each other to give you the best advice. And then they will help you load the car up. Believe me, this is true. I always do it. Not with bricklaying mortar, obviously; in that case I'm the one that's dishing out the advice. But with other things, electrics, plumbing, roofing, I go straight in and say I don't know how to do this, what's the score. Never fails.

Cement, by the way, didn't used to be used in mortar until the 1940s. So if you want to do brickwork repairs to your Victorian house, use sand and lime. Lime mortar sets slowly and retains the ability to move without cracking, which is why some old houses look decidedly lopsided, but don't seem to have any cracks.

Cement mortar is a different proposition. It sets quickly. Rock hard. It will not accommodate any movement whatsoever. Cement mortar plus movement equals cracks. Remember that because I'll be coming back to it later.

Merchants of Doom (30/3/97)

You can buy building materials from four different kinds of retail outlet. Which type you choose can determine quality, price and reliability of advice. There are also covert rules about how you ought to behave in each.

First, your traditional big builders' yard, sometimes part of a chain. Lots of account customers. May be impatient with amateurs. This is partly because the account customers are in there buying seven thousand quid's worth of stuff, and you're in the same queue with one paintbrush and a packet of cup hooks. But it is also because the blokes behind the counter may not actually know any more about building than you do, and are embarrassed by your questions. They are actually just check-out boys, who type or scan in bar codes and print out a computerised receipt. The computer system means that if you want stuff from the yard, cement or bricks, say, you have to get it from the yard man first, who will give you a ticket to take indoors to the counter. Finding the yard man can sometimes be a problem – he is usually hiding in the toilets waiting for the minimum wage to be introduced.

Second, small high street concerns, which in cities are now often run by Asians. These are the builder's equivalent of the local corner shop – they are polite and friendly, good with advice, stock a bit of everything and are open all hours – but they may not be especially cheap. Still, if you want stuff on Sundays and Bank Holidays, which most of us do, they are head and shoulders above the only alternative, the DIY superstores. If you live near an Orthodox Jewish area you may be able to find a builders' merchants open on Sundays, and have the privilege of dealing with a yard man wearing a bowler hat and waistcoat, an experience worth having. The protocol in most of these places is that you pay for everything at the counter first, get your receipt, and then go looking for the yard man. He won't be hiding because he's probably got a stake in the business.

Third, DIY superstores. Only to be used if you're really desperate at eight in the evening. Prices are high and nobody knows anything about anything, whatever the adverts say. Net consumers of time, money, energy, everything. Ghastly places.

Last, but by no means least, are the specialist merchants. General builders' merchants have to stock a bit of everything, so it stands to reason they can't specialise; they will keep a stock of, say, electrical sockets, but only one type. Electrical suppliers, on the other hand, will stock twenty different types of sockets, switches, cable etc, and will know which are the right ones for the job. Same with plumbers' merchants, decorating suppliers, timber yards, architectural ironmongers. The other customers will be specialists, too, and can be a source of invaluable advice. And they are often stunningly cheaper than other outlets – I recently bought an electric shower for sixty quid from my local electrical suppliers, half the price anywhere else. There used to be a problem with specialist suppliers in the boom times of the 'eighties – they only wanted trade account customers, and discouraged DIY-ers. Some of them had signs up saying things like £50 minimum order. But those days are gone. Like cab drivers, they now realise that your money is as good as anyone else's.

Of course, to get trade prices, you are supposed to be 'in the trade'. Don't be shy about this. Make up a company name if they ask you for one. After all, you're doing up your house aren't you? Well then, you're a property developer.

Oh, and by the way, don't ever be tempted to jump the queue at the counter in a builders' merchants, the way you might try to do, say, at the bar of a crowded pub. There are some wild men in the building game, and you wouldn't want to get on the wrong side of any of them.

Decorating for Baby (27/4/97)

Everyone decorates the bedroom for the new baby. It's what you do. New life, new wallpaper. New paint, new carpets, new lights, new curtains. All of these can contain man-made chemicals which may be harmful to health. Health hazards caused by toxins are estimated in proportion to the body weight of the recipient. So an infant weighing, say, four kilograms, will be affected by a dose of contaminant chemical *twenty times* more than an adult weighing 80 kilograms. Is it a good idea to expose new born babies to freshly applied decorating materials? I don't think so. Indoor air pollution is now the subject of widespread research, and a great many decorating and furnishing materials are known to contribute to the total toxic load of any enclosed indoor space.

At last year's 7th International Conference on Indoor Air Quality and Climate, in Nagoya, Japan, papers were presented detailing the effects on health of common indoor air pollutants including solvents, formaldehyde, tobacco smoke, ozone, benzene, insecticides and fungicides. Some of these occur naturally, and are concentrated within homes by the enclosed nature of the built environment; others are artificially introduced in furnishing and decorating materials.

Organic solvents such as white spirit, for example, are the liquid medium used to apply paints, stains, varnishes, adhesives, polishes, damp-proofing fluids and timber treatment chemicals. The solvents are thinner than water, and so can penetrate into porous materials even when they are wet. After application, they evaporate away, having delivered their cargo into place. But this can cause health problems for months afterwards; aside from the intoxicating effects valued by glue sniffers, solvents can damage the nervous system, digestive organs, the heart and circulatory system, the respiratory system, and have been linked with cancer and reproductive hazards. Even water-based paints can present a risk; some of the pigments used to provide the colours are metal-based, and toxic if ingested.

Wallpaper pastes, plasters and plasterboard can all contain fungicides, to inhibit mould growth. Fungicides are toxins, and however small the quantities, they may still represent a health risk in an enclosed space. Many timber products, such as chipboard and MDF (medium density fibreboard) contain formaldehyde, a powerful irritant linked with lung disease, which is also released by a number of foam materials, including cavity wall insulation.

Many homes have been treated with wood preservative chemicals, sometimes more than once. These include fungicides, to prevent rot, and insecticides, against woodworm attack. Even new timber from the builders' merchants may have been chemically treated, as a precaution against moulds and insect damage in transit or storage. Most new carpets, curtain fabrics and furnishings have also been dosed with insecticides, to guard against moth damage in the warehouse.

Insulating materials can also create health problems. Asbestos, of course, is notorious, but man-made fibres, such as those used in mineral wool loft insulation, can cause respiratory problems and even cancer. So, faced with this daunting chemical cocktail, how can you guard against health hazards? Wherever possible, water-based decorating materials should be used rather than solvent-based ones. Ventilation is also important to get rid of the air-born pollutants emanating from any decorating process. And, since many pollutants find their way into the human body via house dust inhaled into the lungs, thorough vacuum cleaning is the single most effective measure against respiratory problems; the Dyson Dual Cyclone system is good at removing the smaller sized particles (including dust mite faeces) which are responsible for most childhood asthma.

But, most importantly, ask yourself why you want to decorate the new baby's room in the first place. Does the new arrival really care what colour the ceiling is? Better to give the place a thorough spring clean and leave the interior decor until the occupant is in a fit state to appreciate it.

Do-it-Yourself (2) (13/7/97)

Most home improvements are nothing of the sort. This is a shame, because people put a great deal of time and effort, not to mention money, into trying to make their homes nicer, better, and more valuable. But, as most home owners discover sooner or later, ten thousand quid's worth of DIY does not turn a £60,000 property into one worth £70,000. It turns it into a £60,000 property with some extra bits stuck on. On occasion, it can even reduce its net worth to £57,750, the difference being the cost of paying a builder to rip out the DIY stuff and dump it in a skip.

On the other hand, a grand's worth of routine maintenance every year could keep a home in first class condition, such that it will fetch the top market price for similar properties in the area. This means things like overhauling the gutters and downpipes, repairing cracked or rotten window sills, replacing slipped or broken slates, and keeping the external joinery clean and painted. Unfortunately these are 'dirty hands' jobs, and might not appeal to your creative home-making urges as much as the latest fad being marketed down at the DIY superstore. DIY marketing promotions will try to persuade you to put up some dado rails instead of oiling your hinges, and to coat your brickwork with a magic colourless waterproofing solution rather than clean the autumn leaves out of your gutters.

Maintenance, clearly, has an image problem, compared with 'home improvement', which is sexy. I suppose if DIY is the new Rock'n'Roll, as was recently suggested in these pages, then cleaning out the drains is the equivalent of playing third cornet with the Brighouse and Rastrick Colliery Band. Serious rockers want to be up there at the creative edge, playing air guitar and rag rolling the kitchen ceiling.

In more sober moments, DIYers build airing cupboards, with hardboard walls and louvred doors. Nobody knows why they are called airing cupboards – they are usually built as tight fitting camouflage boxes around hot water cylinders, so tight that there is never enough room to air much clothing or bed linen. When plumbers dismantle these cupboards, as they have to whenever work is required on the cylinder, they always unearth odd socks, which they then use as golf club covers.

The airing cupboard, by the way, will have a carcass of planed (or PAR – 'planed all round') timber. DIY cupboards and wardrobes always have a carcass of planed two-by-two. No professional carpenter would dream of using this – it is more expensive than rough sawn or 'carcassing' timber, and its dimensions are odd. This is because the two-by-two (inches) measurement is that of the sawn section; the planing reduces it down from that, and often by different amounts in the two directions, depending upon the amount of twist in the wood. But builders' merchants keep a special stock of two-by-two PAR for the Saturday morning DIY crowd.

What else do DIYers do? They screw their floor boards down, that's what. To stop them creaking. This is a bad idea, probably got from the Readers Digest DIY manual. Professionals use cut nails or, more correctly, floor brads; these make it easy to lift and re-fit the boards when doing plumbing or electrical work in the floor voids. Screws, or worse, two inch ovals, are hard to get out, and usually result in split boards. And you know why the replacement boards are always thinner and narrower than the original ones? See planed timber, above.

Education (14/9/97)

Buildings are such simple things to construct and maintain – it's amazing that people find them so bewildering. I mean, be fair, when you get some "builders" round to work on your home, they're not usually your actual white-coated scientist types are they? They're not often what you'd describe as intellectuals. They're just ordinary blokes. In some cases a bit too ordinary – tattoos, fags, beer bellies hanging out of their trousers, racist and misogynist attitudes by the shovelful. Some of these guys have problems reading the *Sun*. So how come you defer to them, and assume they are possessed of secret skills and knowledge that you yourself could not hope to attain?

The problem clearly lies with inadequate education – yours, not theirs. Let's face it, the teachers at your school never came in and said, today, children, we are going to look at roofing. Or plumbing. Or how to choose the right plaster. If they had, then 98% of the population would not be in thrall to the other 2% who have chanced to find out about these things. They would still employ them to do their building work, but they would be more able to tell a good job from a bad one, and would not be so easily duped into having inappropriate or unnecessary work carried out. They would also be able to deal with minor emergencies without getting ripped off.

As I write this, I am looking out across the back gardens at a man sweeping a flood of water off the flat roof of his rear addition. It is a lovely sunny evening, but the water continues to pour down on him. It is coming from the warning pipe, or overflow, from the cistern in his loft. The flat roof is obviously *too* flat because the water is ponding instead of running away into the hopper and downpipe; it is probably seeping back into the brickwork of the main house and appearing as a damp patch inside. So he stands there, in his suit, sweeping, pausing only to look up at the source of the nuisance. I imagine he must have called for help, and he may even have tried the water company. After all, following the recent Drought Summit with that nice Mr Prescott, the water companies agreed to fix everybody's leaks, didn't they? Unfortunately not; the water companies only undertook to mend leaking service pipes, from the company stop valve under the pavement to the rising main inside the property. Leaks in customers' internal plumbing systems remain their own responsibility.

So the man is probably waiting for AAA Plumbing Services out of the Yellow Pages to come and save him. They will charge him £80 for turning up, £35 for turning the water off at the stop valve under the kitchen sink, and £68.73 for replacing the fibre washer on the ball valve in the cistern. Plus VAT. This is a task that the man should be able to do himself in twenty minutes, if only someone had told him how. Instead, he stands there sweeping.

Now, I know what you're thinking. You're thinking, why don't I just nip round and tell the man what to do with his ball valve, and stop all that water being wasted, and save him being fleeced by the emergency plumber. Well, if you must know, it's because of his constantly barking dog, and his recent really loud birthday party that went on till 4 am. And also because, when I thought about it, I remembered he was one of the 98% and I was one of the 2%. Sometimes, we minorities have to stick together.

New Year's Resolutions (4/1/98)

Here, due to popular demand, is your very own Doctor on the House cut-out'n'keep list of New Year's resolutions. Follow these simple steps to keep your home in good order and save money too:

♦ Clean the leaves and sludge out of your gutters, or pay someone else to do it for you. Make sure the gutters are not leaking at the joints, and that they are draining away into an unblocked down pipe. Most of the water threatening your home comes straight down out of the sky, so make friends with your gutters.

♦ Keep the bathroom door closed at all times, and open the window or turn on the extractor fan when bathing or showering. Put a notice on the door instructing other users to do likewise; if they haven't got the message by February, evict them, or fit an automatic door closer and a humidistat-switched fan. These steps will solve most condensation problems, throughout the whole house.

♦ Paint the outside joinery – doors, windows, fascias and barge boards – if they have not been done within the past five years. You are supposed to start by burning off the old gloss paint, but first test it for lead; if there are layers of lead paint then it may be better left undisturbed, and painted over.

♦ Never visit a DIY superstore, except to laugh at the people standing in the enormous check-out queues. Buy your tools and materials at a proper builders' merchants.

♦ Get some decent tools. All homes should have a basic tool kit including a claw hammer, screwdrivers, sharp wood saw, junior hacksaw, pliers, pincers, pipe wrench and adjustable spanner. Optional extras are a 25 mm wood chisel, a plane, and a 50 mm bolster which will double as a floorboard lifter. All these items are best bought individually – don't fall for the "complete tool kit" scam; they are of the cheapest quality and you won't use half of them anyway.

◆   Don't allow anybody to spray nasty chemicals on your floorboards. If you really have got active woodworm – and it is easy to tell – then rejoice; it is a sign that your home is a healthy, non-contaminated place for all life, including your own.

◆   Find out how to programme your central heating. Most importantly, with gas-fired radiator systems, locate the knob that adjusts the temperature of the water leaving the boiler; in winter it is often better to leave the heating permanently on and to turn down the water temperature at night and when you go out. This will help keep surfaces above dewpoint temperature and prevent condensation, which in turn will improve the insulation value of the walls.

◆   Don't even think about replacement double-glazing. If your windows are draughty then first make sure they close properly, and then fit some draught-proofing strip. Use the thousands of pounds that you've saved to get some heavy curtains. Or spend it on a holiday.

◆   Find out how your home works, and you will be less likely to be ripped-off by cowboys and salesmen. There is no one book that covers all you need to know about home maintenance, but *The Penguin Dictionary of Building* explains all the jargon, and contains lots of DIY tips too.

◆   If you need professional advice in 1998, ask a Building Engineer. Call the Association of Building Engineers on 01604 404121 and ask for a list of members in private practice in your area.

◆   Don't panic. You probably know more about building than you think you do.

Garden party (1/2/98)

Writers have a knack of making simple things sound hard. I suppose anything can appear complicated when it is described in prose, but some building publications use photographs and illustrations as well, and still manage to over-elaborate.

For example, leafing through the DIY books and magazines you may easily get the impression that garden walls and paving slabs have to be laid on tonnes of hardcore and concrete. This is rarely the case, and is a typical example of the excesses of modern house building being slavishly promoted for all other circumstances. The main effect of this is to make people think that such tasks are impossibly hard work, or that they can only be done by experienced builders.

Paving certainly involves a bit of healthy physical activity, but it does not have to involve large-scale excavation or the barrowing of loads of concrete. It is usually enough to shovel off the topsoil (saved, to be used later for raised flower beds) and to bed the stone slabs or bricks on 50 mm of coarse sharp sand. Brush sand into the joints as well, and then the rain will be able to drain away through them, without ponding. If any areas of paving subside later on, you can always lift them up and throw a bit more sand underneath, or just leave them and let the whole thing look more ancient. This is the beauty of not using cement or concrete.

On large areas you may want to use a spirit level to guide your removal of the topsoil and the bedding of the slabs, but even this is not essential; a length of string stretched between two sticks will give you a line to work to, and who cares if it's not dead level.

Many people will have been put off trying their hand at bricklaying by DIY books showing deep trenches and concrete foundations. A high boundary wall will need a concrete foundation for stability, but low retaining walls for garden beds can be laid straight onto the subsoil, as walls have been built for thousands of years. Use the string as a guide to level off the ground, and walk up and down it a few times to compact the subsoil. Don't worry if there are soft spots or a bit of topsoil along the line of the wall – for work like this it really doesn't matter. Then bed one brick at each end and stretch the line between them as a guide for the others. You'll soon get the hang of it.

The most important thing is to use bricks which look good and are also going to stand up to the rigours of the weather. This rules out most modern bricks, apart from expensive hand-made ones, and rules in reclaimed bricks from demolition firms. Some people are afraid of demolition men, because they look rough, but most of them are pussy cats underneath. Tell them you want the bricks for garden walls, and they should sell you good hard stocks or wire-cuts that will last longer than your house. Bed them in sand and lime mortar, mixed three to one, using the same coarse sharp sand that you use for your paving.

The next few weeks are your last chance to do building work in the garden, before the plants start getting in the way. So don't be put off by the scare stories – just do it.

Maintenance (1/3/98)

Apparently, in Japan, homes are so expensive that you can get a 200-year mortgage; it's the only way some people can afford a place to live. What a great inheritance from Grandma – a lifetime of debt. Will the old family home still be standing when the last month's repayment has been made?

Which brings us, in a roundabout sort of way, to maintenance. People write in asking about low maintenance, or even "maintenance-free" building products, and I have to say, sadly, that no such thing exists. Everything decays over time; it's simply a matter of how long. For example, uPVC replacement windows are often marketed as being "maintenance free", and so they may be – for 20 years or so – but by then they will have started to embrittle, turn yellow, and the rubber gaskets will leak – a bit like people, really. So anyone aged 60 thinking of putting uPVC windows in their retirement home should be aware that when they are 80 they may have to replace them – at 2018 prices. On the other hand, properly-maintained timber windows – that is, painted three times over that same period – should still be as good as new.

Plastic gutters and drain pipes, too, although they seem to promise zero maintenance, last nothing like as long as their cast-iron predecessors. Some of the latter are still looking good after a century, whilst many of the former are already sagging drunkenly off walls, gushing water from every joint.

Obviously, some materials naturally last longer than others – glass is pretty stable; it just gently flows downwards so that medieval church windows are thicker at the bottom than the top – allegedly. Building lime absorbs carbon dioxide from the air and turns back into limestone, one of the most stable substances on earth. Granite, surprisingly, is not as stable as it looks; some of the granite cladding on the early American skyscrapers is now failing through fatigue, and plummeting down onto the sidewalk. Better check that holiday insurance.

Concrete, too, whilst it looks solid enough, does not have a good performance record over the years. Most notable were the high-alumina concrete disasters of the 1970s, when several schools and swimming pools collapsed without warning; but even ordinary reinforced concrete has been found to decay at an alarming rate – the cement is acidified by carbon dioxide, causing the reinforcing steel to rust.

But when most people yearn for a life free of building maintenance, what they really mean is they don't like painting. External paintwork has the shortest life of any building material, and it should really be burned off and replaced at least every seven years (watch out for lead paint, though – this must never be burned or sanded; but removed only with chemical paint strippers). All external joinery – doors, windows, fascia boards – needs to have its paint system kept intact, otherwise it will get wet and rot; there is no way round it.

When you buy a property you are entering into a contract to maintain it, which is likely to cost you many thousands of pounds, just to keep the place in the same condition as when you bought it. This was not made clear to people during the frenzied home-ownership expansion of the Thatcher years (well, it wasn't an ideal selling point, was it), but the chickens are now coming home to roost. A house is for life, not just for Christmas – maybe there's something in that Japanese system after all.

Double Trouble (6/4/97)

A story in the *Swindon Advertiser* recently described how a local man got so fed up with the persistence of double glazing salesmen that he held one of them hostage in his home until the company agreed to leave him alone. Now, if double glazing is so brilliant, why the hard sell? What, apart from the antics of the salesmen, is wrong with it?

Well, it's not the doubling up of the sheets of glass that is the problem. Twin sheets of glass, with an insulating layer of air trapped between them, are a good idea, and well worth using in new windows in new houses. In an old house, if you were to get all the existing windows re-glazed with twin sheets of glass, or sealed units, as they are known, then you should save money on your heating bill. Whether you would ever actually save enough to cover the cost of the replacement glazing would depend upon how hot you like your home, how cold it is outside, how big the windows are, and whether you live to be 104. It might just be worth it.

No, the trouble with 'double glazing' is that what is actually being marketed under this description is not just the glass but a complete replacement window system. Well, I say complete. Some cowboy operators won't even give you that. They'll simply remove the sliding sashes from your Victorian box frames and screw the replacement window frames into them. You will feel the benefits at first, largely because the new system has cut down on the draughts. But draughts equal ventilation, and if the remaining ventilation is inadequate, which it usually is, then condensation will cause wood rot in the old timber surrounds. So you will be left with new double glazed windows mounted in rotten century-old hollow box frames. Brilliant.

Most replacement windows are made from uPVC. The small 'u' stands for 'unplasticised', as opposed to ordinary PVC which *is* plasticised, which is what raincoats are made out of. But although uPVC is not as bendy as raincoat material, it is still a bit bendy, which is why the frames are so chunky looking. They have to be to stop the whole thing from flopping around when you open it. High quality uPVC frames are stiffened internally with steel strips. Cheap ones may just have steel reinforcement up the sides for fixing to the brickwork, or none at all. The salesman didn't mention that? Well, there's a thing.

Probably the worst scenario with replacement uPVC windows is when the original timber or steel windows had, by accident or design, been supporting some of the weight of the brickwork above. The uPVC is not strong enough to take this load and, after a short time, will start to bend at the top. A characteristic cracking pattern will develop, with a triangle of brickwork detached from the rest of the wall and resting on top of the sagging window frame. This phenomenon can be observed in homes all over the UK, and it is serious bad news for the owners concerned. They have paid thousands of pounds to some chancer who has inflicted serious structural damage upon their homes, and then probably done a runner. Free enterprise; doncha just love it?

Another problem with replacement windows is that they are often 'designed', ha ha, with scant regard for the original glazing pattern, or fenestration. This can knock thousands off the price of a decent Victorian or Edwardian terraced house – the price, in fact, of removing the double glazing and replacing it with the original draughty sliding sash windows.

But the most widespread problem is condensation. Replacement windows tend to make a house airtight, and when that happens condensation follows. Black mould growth in the corners of rooms is the usual first sign, which is an indication of damp walls. Damp walls are poorer insulators than dry walls, so they allow more heat to escape through them. So what was that about double glazing making your heating bills lower?

Roofs (4/5/97)

One of the tragedies of the last eighteen years has been the number of people drawn into home ownership who had no idea of the amount of building maintenance this would involve. Without any previous building knowledge, and suddenly finding themselves responsible for the well-being of a flat or house, many will have fallen prey to unscrupulous builders, or worse – salesmen peddling quack remedies. Such 'instant' home repairs will always have a seductive appeal for the gullible; after all, they offer a *product*, rather than a service; so they appeal to our shopping instincts. The thing is packaged, it is displayed in a glossy brochure, and you can pay for it with your credit card.

Take roof repairs. After replacement double glazing, probably the least sensible item of 'home improvement' is one of the instant roof repair systems on offer. In the past these have taken the form of some kind of externally-applied bituminous coating. The idea of covering your Victorian slate roof with a layer of sticky black goo is contrary to all accepted notions of good roofing practice, to say nothing of accepted notions of making your house look good. The process seals up all the gaps and stops the roof timbers from 'breathing'; this will result in condensation in the roof space, and wood rot in the battens and rafters. It also means that the slates can never be used again. Lately these systems have fallen out of favour, but they have been usurped by methods which, whilst less visually intrusive, can turn out to be just as damaging – internally-sprayed foam coatings. For the uninitiated, these seem to combine a quick-fix repair with the added advantage of insulating the roof at the same time. But the whole thing is a false economy – as well as sealing the roof and stopping it breathing, and hindering the re-use of the slates or tiles, as before – the insulating foam will actually make the rafters and battens colder, and hence speed up the rot.

The reasons people fall for 'instant' roof repairs are common to all building scams – firstly, fear of the expense of getting the job done properly, and secondly, the quality and persistence of the marketing of the product. In addition, roof problems can make us feel particularly vulnerable – `keeping a roof over your head' sums up all sorts of primeval security neuroses, and one slipped slate or tile can result in a frightening intrusion of the elements into our cosy carpeted interiors. Like a flat tyre on the car, getting it fixed becomes the most important thing in our lives. Suppose it cost £100 to get a puncture mended properly at a garage – and £10 for an instant roadside patch-up job? Would we go for the cheap one? You bet we would, even if it only lasted five minutes. (Actually, I may be misjudging human nature here. Some people lavish far more care and attention on their cars than they do on their homes. They may well take the long-term view of car maintenance, even though 'long-term' for a car is – what, two years? Long-term for a house is fifty years, ie. for the rest of your life, so short-termism should really have no place in it.)

Taking care of buildings properly involves more than just shopping for quick-fix products – it requires a rolling programme of care and maintenance which, if undertaken correctly, will be far cheaper than the emergency costs of responding to crises like a slipped slate or a faulty boiler.

Cavity Walls (31/8/97)

Has your house got cavity walls? Or is it built with solid brickwork? Don't be embarrassed if you don't know the answer. Nine out of ten home owners said they hadn't a clue. The information should be in your mortgage valuation report but, hey, who bothers to read that? Like most of the documentation flying around during the house buying trauma, it gets scanned or speed-read down to the bottom line – the one with the £ sign – does the surveyor's valuation meet the asking price, and is the lender going to cough up?

No-one can blame you for that. Buying and selling a home is the third most stressful thing that can happen to you, apparently, after divorce and redundancy, so, understandably, details about your external walls can appear as mere trifles in the wider scheme of things. It may come as some comfort to know that even the anoraks who do read their survey reports can emerge none the wiser. Reports are written in such odd, vague terms that the effect can be like eating a marsh mallow – you remember your jaw going up and down, and the sensation of swallowing, but your stomach offers no evidence of having received any nutrition. Similarly, surveyors' reports can leave a memory of having read something, but no signs of any information having been imparted. This is deliberate. If a surveyor's report contained any actual statements, then it would leave its writer open to legal challenge about their factual basis. And this could present a problem for the writer, and for the writer's professional indemnity insurance premiums. So, in the circumstances, surveyors concur that statements are best avoided. *Appearances* are OK, as in "The walls of the house appear to be built from brick", as are statements attributable to others, like, "The vendors inform us that the roof has been re-slated". And, of course, the many caveats, such as, "Inspection of the floors was not possible owing to the presence of fitted carpets throughout".

Anyway, don't let this put you off. It is important to know if your house has cavity walls, and it is a simple matter to find out. Go outside and look at the brickwork. Are the bricks all the same size and shape, and do they overlap each other by half their length? This pattern is called stretcher bond, and it means the brickwork is 100 mm, or 4 inches, thick. We call this a half-brick wall, and it is usually the outer leaf of a cavity wall. If, on the other hand, it looks as if there are half bricks distributed between the whole bricks, and the bricks overlap each other by a quarter of their length, then you've got Flemish bond or English bond, or some variant of these. What look like half bricks are actually whole bricks turned to run through the depth of the wall. This will be 215 mm or 9 inches thick, and is known as a one-brick wall. It will usually be solid brickwork, with no cavity. If this is your house, you can relax.

If you answered yes to the stretcher bond question, though, you have one further test to carry out. Go back indoors and tap on the inside of the wall. If it sounds hollow, like a wooden box, then you're probably in a timber-framed house, more of which later. If it sounds and feels more solid, then you are, indeed, in a house with cavity walls. For details of how this will affect the rest of your life, see next week's column.

Cavity Walls (II) (7/9/97)

So your house, or the house you are thinking of buying, is one of the 12 million built with cavity walls? You may have been led to believe this is an advantage - that cavity walls are modern and therefore a good thing. Well, don't get me wrong, I'm not against progress. It's just that I've spent twenty years building the things and I've seen what goes on. Give me the solid brickwork of a Victorian house any day. Most architects, incidentally, are the same; they spend their days copying each others' Legoland creations, but they go home in the evenings to nice little Victorian terraced houses in up-and-coming inner city areas.

Now, constructing a brick wall as two separate walls with a gap in the middle may seem like a sound idea, especially if you live in an area with regular heavy driving rain. Houses exposed to such a climate are prone to penetrating damp - that is rainwater lashing against the outsides of the walls, and showing up as damp patches on the insides. It was, in fact, on the Atlantic coast of Ireland where the cavity wall was first widely used, around the 1840s; it then spread to South Wales and the South coast of England. The idea soon caught on, but only in these wet areas; in the dryer climate of London and eastern England builders stuck with the tried and tested stability of solid masonry walls for another hundred years or so. Solid one-brick walls were still being used for housing in London up until the 1950s.

But builders are dedicated followers of fashion, and since the '60s it has become *de rigueur* to use cavity work everywhere. Note, there is nothing in the Building Regulations that says you must have cavity walls - it is simply a fashion thing.

So what's wrong with cavity walls? Well, firstly, since the oil crises of the 1970s, we've become mad keen on thermal insulation, and it was decided, by people who really should have known better, that the cavity would be a neat place to put it. So cavity walls weren't really cavity walls any more, they became solid walls with fluffy spongy stuff in the middle - ideal, in fact, for water to penetrate across from outside to inside. Secondly, modern cavity walls are impossible for bricklayers to build properly; they contain lots of extra metal and plastic bits, designed to hold the thing together, keep the heat in, and ... er ... keep the penetrating damp out. This has reduced bricklaying from a creative art to the assembling of a kit of parts. Half of them get left out, or put in the wrong place - believe me. Surveys by the Building Research Establishment have found the overwhelming majority of faults reported in new houses concern badly-built external cavity walls.

And thirdly, the inner and outer leaves of cavity walls are held together with metal wall ties. This is important to know because, at some stage, someone is going to try and tell you, or the person who wants to buy your house, that your cavity wall ties are rusty and need replacing. In many cases this will not be true; wall tie corrosion has become the latest thing that surveyors draw attention to in case they get sued for not drawing attention to it. But if your house was built between 1964 and 1981, it will probably have very thin, poorly galvanized steel wall ties, which will eventually need replacing. Still, look on the bright side; at least you didn't buy your council flat ... did you?

A Touch of the Sun (17/8/97)

Most building defects come to light when the cold and wet are involved, so it may come as a surprise to hear that hot weather can bring its share of problems too. These usually centre around thermal expansion – which means that as things get hotter they get bigger – and drying shrinkage, which means that as things get hotter they get smaller. It would be handy if these two were to cancel each other out but, with building as with life, that would be too much to hope for. On the contrary, the two effects can combine to make things worse – such as when a steel hinge expands at the same time as the window frame to which it is screwed is shrinking – these conflicting movements will result in stress and, as the song says, something's gotta give.

So, thermal expansion is most significant for dry things like metals and plastics, and drying shrinkage affects materials containing water – notably timber – but also concrete, mortar and plasters, especially if they are being mixed and used in hot weather conditions.

Probably the most common thermal expansion problem involves black uPVC guttering. This stuff expands and contracts more than any other building material, which is why you can hear it creaking and clicking as it swells in the sunshine – and as it shrinks when a cloud passes over. As the temperature rises from 15°C to 35°C – which has been happening across the country every day for the past week – a 10 m length of uPVC guttering will expand by 10 mm. And in the cool of the evening it will try to shrink back by the same amount. Note, I say "try" – the plastic support brackets are marked with lines indicating a recommended expansion gap between lengths – unfortunately this is sometimes misunderstood or ignored by the people who put the stuff up, so the first summer's expansion simply pushes the whole length along to the point of least resistance, which can actually move the running outlet – the funnel bit – clean away from the downpipe. You won't notice this, of course, until a sudden thunderstorm strikes, and you've got a roof's worth of rainwater cascading down one point of the wall. Some people don't even seem to notice cataclysmic events like this, until the constant soakings start to show through on the inside of the bedroom wall. Then they think the house has contracted a mysterious disease called "damp".

Even when guttering is fixed according to the instructions it still may not shrink back into its rightful position, because of silt washed off the roof into the expansion gaps. Interlocking concrete roof tiles are the worst offenders here – they can erode at an alarming rate, accelerated by the mosses and lichens that love to take root on them. So the guttering expands, but it cannot contract; it gets progressively shoved along in its brackets by what is known as the ratchet effect, until, somewhere along the line, something pops out of place, and another "damp" disaster is poised to occur.

The ratchet effect can also be observed on chimney stacks, whose exposed positions mean they bear the brunt of both thermal and moisture movement. Gaps open up between the bricks, and the situation is often made worse by over-enthusiastic pointing up with sand and cement mortar. The result is the stack can only get bigger, and never shrink back again.

So remember, if cracks appear in the summer, it may just be a touch of the sun; wait to see if the change is permanent before reaching for the pointing trowel or the filler tub.

Cracking Up (24/8/97)

Buildings move. They don't move around town or go to discos or anything like that, but they do expand and contract in response to heat and moisture and vibration. And when you apply loads to them, like going inside, they sink a bit. And when you come out they pop back up again. Amazing but true. When a sparrow lands on a steel railway bridge its weight causes movement; difficult to measure, but real nonetheless.

Subsidence is the movement problem that attracts most publicity, and most of what is written about it is nonsense. Subsidence first hit the headlines when, due to a little-noticed change in the regulations, it become the subject of buildings insurance claims after the dry summer of 1976. As usual when the insurance industry gets involved, it didn't take long for the sound of sledgehammers cracking nuts to be heard – in this case with an accompanying chorus of chainsaws. Trees, it was decided, were the problem because they suck water out of the clay and cause shrinkage and subsidence, so they should not be allowed to grow within 30 metres of buildings. This will come as a surprise to the regulars at my favourite pub, the Low House in Laxfield, Suffolk. The pub has been there for six hundred years and, for the last couple of centuries at least, a huge sycamore tree has been trying to gain unauthorised admission to the tap room. The tree is now over two metres wide, and within a whisker of achieving its objective, but still there are no signs of cracking in the building.

The problem with modern buildings is they are unable to tolerate this sort of movement or, come to that, any sort of movement. They are built using techniques and materials that work fine so long as nobody breathes or slams the door. Take any 1990s house, lower one corner by 10 mm, and cracks will appear: in the face brickwork; in the plasterboard ceilings; around the window frames; across the internal plaster. A house built in the 1890s, on the other hand, accommodates that sort of shift without a murmur. I have worked on Victorian houses that have suffered five, six, ten times that amount of movement – houses where the door openings have become trapezoidal, and the pianola has to be tethered to stop it rolling across the parlour floor – and not a crack to be seen. These buildings remain flexible. They are made from bricks bedded in lime mortar; they have lime and horsehair plaster on the walls; the window and door frames are wedged in generous rebates in the brickwork; and the timbers are chunky sections of closely-grained heartwood, still full of preserving pine resin.

Anyway. Every dry summer since 1976 has seen a growing rash of insurance claims for subsidence and remedial underpinning. The construction industry responded to this with its customary free market flexibility, and hundreds of specialist underpinning firms appeared in the Yellow Pages. These gave the insurance industry what it was looking for – three estimates – and so the 1980s underpinning phenomenon was born. Every time a mortgage valuation surveyor south of a line from the Humber to the Severn spotted a hair line crack, he recommended getting a structural engineer's report, and most of these specified underpinning. For a few years things went a bit crazy. I've seen back additions underpinned; I've seen one half of a pair of semis underpinned; I have even – note this – seen a terraced house, in the middle of a row of five, underpinned. Still, I shouldn't grumble; some of us got big drinks for keeping quiet about that one.

Estimating (27/7/97)

My neighbours have decided to have a conservatory built. So they have done the right thing, or what all their friends have told them is the right thing, and asked three builders for estimates. Trouble is, they got the three builders round and said, how much for a conservatory over here? So they've now got three estimates for three different builders' ideas of what constitutes a conservatory – how can they tell which one is going to be the best bet, in terms of quality and value? They can't. Because they didn't have a drawing, or even a written description, for the builders to work on. They just said, see this bit of back yard here, well we want a conservatory on it. Now, there are conservatories and conservatories. Brick walls or timber? With or without concrete foundations? Double or single glazing? Timber frames or uPVC? Glass roof or corrugated polystyrene?

You can't really ask a builder to estimate for a job unless you provide a drawing and some kind of specification. Well, within reason, that is. I mean, if you ask someone round to clean the leaves out of your gutters, you shouldn't have to provide him with a drawing of the gutters. Mind you, with some of the characters going round calling themselves builders these days, you sometimes wonder if that might not be a bad idea.

No, seriously, for maintenance items like that, or getting a ceiling plastered, you should be able to rely upon a simple verbal description. Note, of course, that your verbal description of the work, and the builder's verbal estimate, constitute a verbal contract, which is just as binding, in the eyes of the law, as a written one. So even with small jobs like this, be careful what you say, or it could lead to arguments. You will know from your own observations at the DIY superstore that a door, for example, can cost £30, for the hollow plywood version, or £300, for the solid hardwood panelled job. So if you ask a builder to give you a price for supplying and fitting a new door, you'd be crazy not to give some thought as to what kind of door you both have in mind.

Brickwork is another example. Punters get you round and say, how much for a garden wall? I can get you bog standard London Brick Company Flettons for £120 a thousand, but I wouldn't be seen dead with them around my garden; they look naff and the frost will blow their faces off within a few years. Second hand yellow stocks cost £350 per thou, but they look great and they'll still be standing in fifty years' time.

But it's not just appearance – things that get built without regard to the correct design procedures can present more serious problems. I was once asked to repair some cracks in the brickwork where a rear addition had been built onto a house. One glance told me what the problem was – the rear addition didn't have any foundations. Really. The bricks had been laid straight on top of the patio paving slabs. The thing was slowly sinking under its own weight, and falling away from the house. Well, there's no point trying to repair the cracks in that sort of situation – the thing needed pulling down and rebuilding properly. Unfortunately they'd just had it rewired and plumbed, and it had fifteen thousand quid's worth of Poggenpohl kitchen in it. They asked me what could they do. Hide the crack with a climbing plant and sell the house, I ventured. So they did. A hundred and eighty grand. The buyers' surveyor didn't spot a thing.

Modern Times (21/9/97)

There is much talk of modernising at present – modern democracy, modern monarchy. What does it mean? In architecture they started talking about the modern movement in the 1930s, and got stuck with it. So now if you talk about modern buildings to architects they think you're referring to ones sixty years old and falling to bits. Tip to budding authors: never use the word modern in your title – it will look stupid in a surprisingly short space of time.

But there are huge commercial interests trying to get you to "modernise" your home, and estate agents are their apologists, as in, "This interesting period property, in need of complete *modernisation* ..." Never mind that over the years modernisation has implied the introduction of asbestos cement sheeting, organo-chlorine timber treatments and polystyrene ceiling tiles – things we now can't wait to remove from our buildings – we are currently inveigled to install uPVC double glazing, plastic guttering and MDF kitchen worktops, all things that the next generation will have to remove and dispose of.

Still, these may come to be seen as minor amendments to buildings compared with the major structural alterations of the

1960s that came to be known as the "knocking through" movement. Knocking through meant totally or partially removing the spine wall of the standard British home, be it Victorian terrace or 1930s semi, so that the front room and the back room became one. In my family, anyway, they were called the front room and the back room. Older people called the front room the parlour, and in company ours was sometimes called the sitting room. At some indeterminate point in the mid '60s it became the lounge, and then it disappeared altogether because it was knocked through into the dining room, to suit the trend for open plan living.

Almost every house in every street in every British town was subjected to this ritual disembowelment between 1960 and 1975. The technique was crude but quick – prop the floor above on half-a-dozen Acrows, bash out the one-brick-thick spine wall with a lump hammer, brick up the reveals and slide an RSJ in to pick up the joists. In quite a few cases the debris – plaster, mortar and broken brick – were not even taken off the premises; a couple of floor boards were lifted and the whole lot was shovelled underneath, where it remains to this day.

Nowadays you're not allowed to treat buildings like this, not since the insurance companies started getting hip to claims for cracks in buildings. Because if you just knock out a load-bearing wall like that, you transfer the load to the smaller areas of foundation that remain at the sides, and the increased stress on those areas can mean settlement and building movement. So now, if you remove a wall, you have to replace it with an over-designed steel frame to ensure the even spread of the loading down to the ground.

Needless to say, the smart move now is to buy a "modernised", knocked-through period property and restore it to its original form, rebuilding the spine wall and giving yourself two downstairs rooms instead of one, not to mention all that extra wall area for your Ikea shelving. But why did knocking through become so fashionable in the first place? Personally I blame American sitcoms. We saw the Lucy Show and we thought the Yanks all lived in huge open plan living rooms with a staircase going up the back. We didn't realise it was just a TV studio. The greatest American architectural influence on Britain wasn't Frank Lloyd Wright, it was Dick Van Dyke.

Sins of our Fathers (25/1/98)

"We've all been there; we've all done it", grunts Bethnal Green Eddie as he pulls the runner along the batten, carving another short length of cornicing from the wet lime putty. We are talking about the damage inflicted in the name of "modernising" old houses.

How could anyone have been so shortsighted as to hack the plaster mouldings off a Victorian ceiling? It's costing me a fortune to put them back; BGE is not ripping me off – it just takes hours and hours of tedious, messy work. The lime has been slaking in a big plastic tub for a week, and is now the colour and consistency of double cream. Eddie ladles a dollop into a small bowl, and stirs in a dash of casting plaster (plaster of Paris).

The casting plaster starts to set in a few minutes, so timing is critical; the lime is trowelled onto the ceiling, and the shaped metal runner is slid along a timber batten nailed to the wall, pulling the stiffening lime mix roughly into shape. Then it's scraping all the tools clean and repeating the process three or four times, building up the cornice in layers; and then moving a metre along the wall and starting on the next stretch. It's a slow old business.

When the cornices were first run in, in 1872, the guy was getting tuppence an hour; BGE's hourly rate is somewhat higher, which is why it is easy to get annoyed with whoever it was chopped the things down in 1972. And today I am feeling especially irritated with this unknown previous owner, because I have just discovered what he did with the marble fireplace out of the front room.

Having written a piece for these pages only recently on the virtues of a tidy entrance, I determined to put this one in order, so while Eddie was busy cornicing in the hallway, I was out front, breaking up the patch of crumbling concrete which the estate agent humorously described as the front garden. I started levering the slab up with a pick, breaking it with a lump hammer, and bucketing it to the skip. The concrete was weak, thin stuff laid on an uneven bed of hardcore. In fact the hardcore was proving more effort to pick out than the concrete; it was broken red bricks mostly – probably the missing chimney breast, another favourite target for the modernisers. But then I came across a cube of smooth white stone mixed in with the powdery brick. And then another, and another, this time with a curved edge and traces of carved detail. It couldn't be, could it? Surely, not even in the dark days of the 1970s could anyone have been so stupid as to smash up fine Sicilian marble to use as hardcore. But there it was, spread over one corner of the front garden, 500 quid's worth of mid-Victorian fireplace – columns, corbels, mantle, the lot. I was so disheartened I had to stop; the very thought of chucking it in the skip was depressing me. So I went indoors to share my grief with Eddie.

He's right. We've all done it, and people continue to do it - fireplaces, slates, sash windows, cornices – and whatever the age of the house it's always a mistake. I mean, whoever thought 1960s houses would become "period properties"? – but it's happening. Keep your home as close as you can to its original condition, and one day it will pay you back.

Robbing the Past (22/3/98)

If you're doing up an old house then you'll want to use second-hand materials to match the period feel of the original, right? Well, wrong, actually, according to the Society for the Protection of Ancient Buildings. SPAB are very keen for period features to be retained and restored – but preferably in the properties in which they were originally used. They believe that using materials salvaged from one old house to restore another actually *encourages* demolition and, more depressingly, theft.

There is no doubt that there is a thriving trade in reclaimed materials and fixtures, from fireplaces and floorboards to bricks, chimney pots and even complete staircases. And when free trade detects a demand, there will always be someone willing to supply – legally or otherwise. The illegal end of the market is clearly encouraged by the premium on easily-shifted items such as fireplaces; a mid-Victorian marble surround can be removed in a matter of minutes, and can fetch an easy £500. At the legal end a builder or property developer can remove and sell antique bricks or roof tiles for a pound apiece, and replace them with modern factory-made ones costing 25 pence; if the building is unlisted, then it's all perfectly legitimate.

So SPAB's view is that if the trade in second-hand building materials was outlawed, these items would cease to have a monetary value and would have more chance of staying in their original homes. You may think this view is a bit simplistic. What about, for example, the case of an old building that has to be demolished anyway, to make way for a new airport (yuck – OK, hospital then); is it not A Good Thing that the materials should be re-used to give a fresh lease of life to other old buildings – just like organ transplants? A tricky one, that; but when you think about it, any such dispensation would leave a loop-hole for the unscrupulous. Conservation officers have to cope with this every day, from unscrupulous contractors who "accidentally" knock down old buildings and trees by backing trucks into them.

But if the salvage trade was stopped, where would you go for replacement bricks and tiles to match your existing ones? Simple, say SPAB – if the demand is there, then people will go back to making materials using the old methods. At present, hand-made bricks and tiles are more expensive than second-hand ones, but if demand increased then unit costs should fall; and we would be encouraging people to take up these dying skills, re-creating local jobs. And what about the new materials standing out visually against the weather-beaten old originals? Well, if they are made using traditional materials and methods, then they should soon blend in, and, say SPAB, the repair will be more architecturally and historically honest than one using cannibalised bits from other buildings.

This is an interesting debate, and one which deserves more attention. Our building heritage is under increasing threat as it is, from the pebble-dashers and double-glazers. So it is a sobering thought that even people who thought they were safeguarding old buildings by using salvaged materials, may have been unwittingly making things worse.

Have you ever seen those bonfires of elephant tusks, aimed at wiping out the ivory trade? Perhaps a few public crushings of Suffolk pantiles would have a similar effect on the trade in stolen building materials.

Barn Storm (13/4/97)

I have made an appearance on the new Channel 5 programme 'Hot Property'. I am the guest expert. On the converted barn. Not a lot to say, really, outside of the obvious. Barns were built for animals, and houses were built for humans. If you had suggested to a farm labourer a hundred years ago that if he was a good boy and stacked all his hay and sowed all his oats he might one day get to live in the barn, you might have considered yourself fortunate to escape with a strategically-placed thrust of his pitchfork.

But not now. Barns are where it's at. The rotting carcass version starts at around sixty grand, and the finished article can command a cool quarter of a million. And the locals just cannot believe it. This is not solely due to rural philistinism; real country folk have an understandably pragmatic *penchant* for centrally heated council houses; come on, if you spent your life before the plough you would too.

But the locals wouldn't live in a barn because they know the pitfalls. First, location. Or, as Estate Agents say, location, location and location. Barns were built on farms. They are hardly ever on their own, and are usually within a few metres of the farmhouse. The farmhouse may have been gentrified and now occupied by a retired civil servant, or it may still be a farmhouse, in which case it will start getting noisy at around five every morning, with chickens, tractors, compressors, grain dryers and the other essential *accoutrements* of modern rural life. The farm labourers' tied cottages will be within pitchfork-throwing distance, too. Again, these may now be picturesque holiday homes, or they may have been replaced with council houses.

People who live in converted barns always talk about the draughts. Barns are draughty because they are big; even if tightly sealed against the weather, the size of the place encourages internal convection currents, which gently waft the heat away from the occupants and up into the roof space.

And few barn conversions do achieve the task of keeping out the elements. The timber frames move, expanding with warmth and moisture, and contracting with cold and dryness. Very few infill materials are able to accommodate this movement – wattle and daub was pretty successful for a few thousand years, having similar thermal and moisture characteristics to the timber – but it has recently fallen out of favour, probably because you can't buy it in bags from B&Q. All the modern equivalents create problems: polyurethane foam boards, plasterboard, plaster on metal lathing – they are all too rigid and immovable. The constant movement of the timber frame will separate it from these adjoining panels, leaving gaps for the draughts.

The other enemy of the modern barn conversion is wood rot. Ironically, it goes hand-in-glove with keeping out the draughts; the old barns lasted for centuries because they were so well ventilated, but seal them up and they can rot within months. This is most commonly observed when new brick or stone plinths, complete with damp-proof courses, are built up underneath the old timber wall plates (the beams at ground level). The new masonry traps moisture up against the wood and rot quickly follows.

Many builders anticipate this and make a pre-emptive strike, dosing the timber with chemicals. This is not a clever move; if you have damp timber and you drench it with toxic chemicals then you end up with, ... er, damp timber drenched with toxic chemicals. Believe it or not, mortgage lenders ask for 'guarantees' that this pantomime will keep the rot at bay for the next 25 years. Now if, a hundred years ago, you'd asked the farm labourer how best to stop the barn from rotting, ... well, you'd be used to dodging the pitchforks by then.

Home on the Range (20/4/97)

The term 'cowboy' has come to signify an untrained worker, especially in the building industry. But the original cowboy builders were actually real Wild West cowboys, who earned their keep during the winter months, when there were no cattle drives going on, by doing odd jobs around the farmstead. There are no records to suggest that their manual dexterity or attention to detail were any less than those of other men. After all, you'd think that anyone who could saddle a horse, ride the range, and hog-tie a steer – whatever that means – could probably make a decent fist of putting up some shelves. The true modern equivalent of the cowboy is the farmworker who constructs and repairs agricultural buildings, most of which do not appear to be any the worse for it.

A recent discussion on site revealed that one of the labourers was a sculptor, and another a script writer. This is not unusual; as a bricklayer I have been kept supplied with mortar and bricks by teachers, solicitors, musicians and, on one memorable occasion, by a Portuguese opera singer. The building industry is a bit like the French Foreign Legion – people come to it from all kinds of backgrounds, with no questions asked. Some stay, others move on. There are always plenty of students, of course, and on site they get to rub shoulders with men with prison records; they all look the same – tattoos, earrings, ripped jeans – only by their speech can you tell them apart; the ex-cons are far more articulate. Once I was on a site when the foreman announced he had to take the next day off to appear in court – "Speeding?" I asked sympathetically; "Attempted murder", he replied, quietly.

Building work is like no other occupation. Where else, these days, can you turn up at the gate and offer your labour and be taken on, on the spot, and given a chance? To that extent the organisation of building work is a survivor from the agricultural and manufacturing work practices of years gone by. These other industries have moved on, in terms of skills and the size of the workforce. But building has remained roughly the same. The itinerant workers who used to turn up at docks and farms and factory gates can now really only turn up at building sites. If they can do the job they'll stay; if not, they'll be down the road by tea time. Qualifications, or the lack of them, don't really come into it. Nobody ever asks; it could lead to arguments. Most people can understand being sacked for making a mess of something – the evidence is usually pretty damning – but being refused work for lack of a certificate? Well, it just doesn't happen. It used to, when building workers were actually employed by contractors, but the past 18 years have seen the demolition of that system, so that everyone is now self-employed.

The Construction Industry Training Board (CITB) has recently approached the qualifications issue by starting up the Construction Skills Certification Scheme (CSCS). Workers with existing construction qualifications, like City and Guilds, qualify automatically, as do unqualified but experienced workers, who get in under 'grandfather rights' if a contractor will vouch for their abilities. From later on this year, all new entrants to the scheme will need to have an NVQ (National Vocational Qualification). The scheme is a laudable attempt to tackle the qualifications vacuum in the construction industry; unfortunately, as long as everyone remains self employed, its effects will remain peripheral. Standards in the industry will only really improve when building workers are given proper conditions of employment, with training, sick pay, holidays and pensions.

But in case you were starting to despair about the lack of qualifications in the building industry, take comfort in the proposed joint honours degree in Building Surveying and Equine Studies (yes, really) at Northampton. This is clearly designed to appeal to a different class of cowboy.

Timekeeping (22/6/97)

When I told a woman at a dinner party that I was a builder, she gave me a funny look and said "Why do builders never turn up?" Good question. But I could ask the same about office workers; whenever I phone the council or the building society and ask to speak to the person I dealt with last time, it seems they're either off sick, on a course, or in a meeting. So why should builders be any different?

Another example. When you buy a house, you think nothing of the fact that the conveyancing process takes three or four weeks, when the actual paperwork involved could be completed by the solicitor's secretary in a morning; so why complain that your plumber takes three weeks to fit the shower? He'll be working at a similar rate – doing several small jobs consecutively for different punters.

Now, there are two ways of paying builders. One is to pay an hourly or daily rate, and the other is to get the whole job done for a fixed price. You might think that the first option would result in more disputes about timekeeping – but not so. The most serious breakdowns in the builder/client relationship occur with price work, and I have a theory why this is. It's all about control. When you employ a builder on a day rate, you are effectively his employer – if he doesn't turn up, he doesn't get paid; if he doesn't work hard enough, you have the right to look disapprovingly at him, make tut-tutting noises, or reduce his biscuit ration.

Builders in the real world, by the way, don't get paid for tea breaks or lunch. Eight till five counts as an eight hour day, with half hour breaks at 10 and 12.30. Make sure your builders abide by these rules, and there's one less thing to fall out about. Of course, this does rather cast you into the role of foreman, which many punters don't fancy; hence the initial attraction of price work.

Because when the job is being done for a price, you can relax and let the builder get on with it – or can you? Well, apparently, no. You no longer have any direct financial control over the work and, therefore, there is a loss of power. This can manifest itself in mysterious ways. The punter still wants to be the centre of the builder's attention, and wants him to turn up every day until the job is finished. But the builder can make a start on the job and, secure in the knowledge that the punter will not be able to exercise any further control over its progress, is free to go out and start organising the next job, and the one after that. It's an inevitable consequence of self employment – the small builder or tradesman cannot devote himself fully to one job at a time – if he did, then when it finished he'd have nothing to go on to. He has to be his own surveyor, estimator, negotiator, secretary and bookkeeper – the amount of time he can actually be at your house, doing the work, is limited.

Some clients just can't handle this. They think they own you, and want you to devote yourself exclusively to them. Bethnal Green Eddie went for a tea break the other day, and his client (a famous TV actor, as it happens), spotting him in the cafe, charged in and made a scene. This was a bad move – the finishing date for his job, uncertain at the best of times, now looks likely to be further disrupted by the millennium celebrations.

Pig (3/8/96)

There is more to this bricklaying business than meets the eye. Before starting on the walls of a house, the brickie positions the frame for the door. A good bricklayer will get to the top of the frame with an exact number of brick courses. This is achieved by changing the thickness of the bedding mortar, to alter the depth of each course of brickwork – known in the trade as gauging.

Modern bricks are 65 mm deep, and laid on a 10 mm mortar

bed, giving a nominal gauge of 75 (I won't bother with the "mm" bit from now on; if you don't know why then you havn't been paying attention.) Now, suppose your door frame measures 2150 to the top of the head of the frame. If you divide that by 75, the depth of one course of brickwork, you get 28-and-a-half-and-a-bit courses, which clearly will not do. The brickwork will finish higher than the door frame. So, a bricklayer will adjust the gauge, either thickening the bed joints, giving 22 courses of 77 and six courses of 76 – 28 courses in total – or better still, tightening them up to give 25 courses of 74 and four courses of 75 – a total of 29 courses. Got that? Good, I'll be asking questions later.

The point is, working out the gauge requires a fair bit of numerical ability. It is no joke to say that to be any good at the job, a brickie needs to know his 75 times table. It was even harder with the old imperial measurements – bricks used to be two and five-eighths inches deep, laid on three-eighths inch bed joints, a gauge of three inches. So, you mental arithmetic gymnasts, how would you gauge your brick courses to get to the top of a 6 foot 10 inch frame?

That is why bricklayers used to be held in such high esteem, not just on building sites, but in working-class society in general. The old brickies had to be numerate, literate and articulate, the cream of the construction trades; only the most intelligent working-class boys would be given the chance of a bricklaying apprenticeship. Look back at the 1914 City and Guilds exam papers for Advanced Craft bricklaying, and you will see questions that would baffle many of today's Civil Engineering undergraduates. And now? Now bricklaying is looked down upon, as a job fit only for morons and no-hopers. People who cannot do anything else are sent to institutions and made to pick up a trowel.

Anyway, when you're working on a really big prestigious brickwork job, like some of the architectural award winning piles thrown up in London's Docklands in the 'eighties, you've got maybe thirty bricklayers doing different bits of the building. Often you get moved around from day to day, so one day you're on the south west corner – next day you're on the north east corner. Well, what can happen is that the gauge on the different corners gets out of sync – you end up with say, 215 courses on one corner and 216 on another. The only way to connect them up, and leave the brickwork level at the top, is to cut a sloping course of bricks with hammer and chisel, from 75 at one end, down to 0 at the other. This is known as a course of pig, and some very famous architects would be amazed if they knew how often this has happened on their own prize-winning buildings. For further information, postal orders to the usual address please.

Garden Wall (20/7/97)

You wouldn't believe how ignorant some people are about building. Last week I went to price up this job for a garden wall. Lovely garden; lawns, rose beds, shrubs, the lot. Bungalow; single lady; fifty-something; two yapping dogs. I can cope with that, but, apparently, the neighbours can't. The neighbours are complaining about the dogs getting into their garden, *via* the twin-strand wire boundary fence. So she's decided to build a wall.

Now, the trouble here is you get drawn into the dispute with the neighbours. And it's the worst kind of dispute – it concerns, one, territory and two, mummy's little boys, the aforementioned yapping brothers. I should have known better. I should have turned round and driven off as soon as I heard the things barking. No, I should have turned round when I saw the bungalow. I should have known from the post code. I should never have been a bricklayer in the first place; there must have been a mix up at the hospital.

Anyway. It was a lovely evening. I pulled up outside the bungalow and the car was immediately surrounded by the two dogs. I opened the car door bravely and pretended I liked being ... I think the term is *worried*. The dogs worried me to the front door. The lady and the dogs worried me to the back garden, and I was shown a beautifully tended border shrubbery, and the two strands of wire, and next door's equally meticulous border, and I was asked to price up for a boundary wall. God, I can't believe I was so stupid. I was there for an hour and a half. I gave her all the options, and in the end we decided upon half-brick panels topped with stone copings, 750 high, with brick-and-a-half piers every four metres. And all the while the dogs were growling and snapping at my legs – that is when they weren't dashing next door to tear up the lawn and squash the geraniums.

So I finally got the thing measured up, and started working out a price. Remove top soil, level bottom of trench, place concrete foundation – that sort of thing. That's what you have to do if you're building a proper garden wall – you have to take the load down to a level below which the frost won't expand it and the summer drought won't shrink it. Otherwise it will start to move and crack. So I said to Miss Two Mutts, "Do you want me to price for moving the shrubs, or would you prefer to look after them yourself?"

You could have heard a pin drop. Even the dogs fell silent. "Move?" "Shrubs?" I could sense from her tone, not to mention her body language, that I had said the wrong thing. The growling started up again, but this time it was more menacing, as though the previous growling had just been messing about. "You can't move the shrubs – they're established."

I tried to explain that she had asked me to price for a wall, and a wall needs a foundation, and anyway the bricklayer has to walk up and down when he's building the wall and there's going to be bricks and mortar and mess and ... do you know what she said – she said "can't you build a sort of platform over them?"

And then it became clear. She didn't really want a wall. Not a brick wall, anyway. She wanted a metaphorical wall between her and the neighbours. Preferably one which made the neighbours evaporate. If I could build those, I tell you, I could clean up.

Builders Behaving Nicely (8/2/98)

How do you get hold of a decent builder? This is a frequently-asked readers' question, and one to which there are no ready answers. The usual advice is to ask your friends to recommend one, but this must be a long shot – unless your friends are themselves construction experts, who are they to judge whether the work done is good, appropriate, or was even necessary in the first place? Friends' recommendations are most likely to produce builders who turn up, feed the cat when you're away, and don't smoke or read *The Sport*. All very nice, but hardly a testament to the quality of their work.

In fact, nice middle-class builders can be a pain. They drink Earl Grey tea, which means they'll help themselves to yours; they read big newspapers, and so need extended tea breaks; and they engage you in meaningful discussions about human rights in Burma, Gordon Brown and, worst of all, their personal relationship problems. This is all down time as regards getting the work done; no wonder your friends recommended them – it was the only way to get them out of their kitchen and into someone else's. Proper prole builders buy their own tea in polystyrene cups from the cafe, look at the pictures in the tabloids, and if they discuss anything with you at all it will be football and/or the Spice Girls. Still no guarantee of quality work, though.

Another common bit of advice is to choose a member of a trade association, but this doesn't necessarily count for much – most trade associations exist to protect their members from the public, rather than the other way round. I was recently in need of a plumber, the boy Steve being tied up until 2006, so I asked the Heating and Ventilating Contractors' Association for details of three members in my area, and called them. One didn't turn up, another told me that water couldn't be pumped downwards, so I couldn't have a radiator in the hall, and the third paid hardly any attention to the details of the job but kept asking if I could pay cash. If anyone from the HVCA wants to tell me these three were an exception to their otherwise impeccable standards then I will listen, but the obvious assumption must be that this association does not monitor its members' behaviour.

So how to control standards of building work? In many countries you cannot offer yourself for work in the building trades unless you have appropriate qualifications and are registered with a government scheme; but successive British administrations have resisted calls for this. The middle-class professions have protected titles – you can't just call yourself an architect, for example – but anyone else can say they're a plumber or a plasterer.

Against this background, I offer a tentative welcome to a scheme being started by ICI/Dulux to police the standards of painters and decorators using their materials. Members of Dulux Trade Select are supposed to follow a code of practice which includes fair prices, written quotes and quality of work. The customer and decorator both complete a registration card for the job and Dulux offer a 12 month guarantee on the work.

This sounds like the sort of control that should be exercised over all the building trades, and in the absence of any government scheme, Dulux's initiative is to be applauded. I shall look forward to hearing readers' comments on whether it is successful.

Doctor Doctor (29/3/98)

When you go to the doctor, you naturally want to know that he or she is a proper, trained, qualified doctor, who has spent a few years studying and then had a bit of supervised experience before being let loose on the general public. You don't demand to see the certificates before you make an appointment, but you are pretty sure that, if you asked, certificates could be produced. You are confident that there are rules and regulations – laws, even – that prevent any old Tom, Dick or Harry setting themselves up as a GP. It's the sort of thing that government is for, isn't it – using tax money for training and registration, to protect the · public. It's the same with dentists, solicitors, accountants. Architects, even.

So why is the government so reluctant to introduce a registration scheme for builders? After all, homeowners spend thousands of millions of pounds annually on building work, and usually have no idea whether the builders who do it have so much as a cycling proficiency badge to their name. There is nothing to stop anyone turning up at your house and saying, I'm a builder, give me some money and I'll do some work for you.

This lack of training and qualifications results in a number of common errors. One such is the raising of outside ground levels by laying new paths and patios on top of old ones – builders who do this do not realise that they are increasing the risk of dampness inside. The use of strong cement mortars to repair or re-point old brickwork is another; very few builders have any idea that this can cause serious long-term damage. Replacement double-glazed windows, chemically-treated timbers, silicone water-repellants – all these things have implications for the health of a building and its occupants, so is it right that they should be specified and installed by someone who has picked up his building knowledge down at the pub? But that's what happens.

Recently, a chance to rectify the situation seemed to present itself. Constructionline is the name of a register of building contractors and consultants approved by the DETR for use in the public sector. It had been hoped by many of us that the register would be extended to the private sector and, in time, to the domestic building market – builders would be screened for their qualifications and financial propriety, and their performance checked on a regular basis; at last, a real opportunity to weed out the cowboy builders.

So what happened? First of all, the government decided that membership of the scheme should only be voluntary – a mandatory system would be, they say, anti-competitive. And secondly, the concession to administer Constructionline is to be sold to a private company. The Chartered Institute of Building applied and were turned down, and none of the five firms shortlisted has any connection whatsoever with the building industry – they are mostly computer services organisations. These outfits may be good at compiling databases, but are they best-placed to decide whether Fred the builder knows how to deal with a flat roof problem on a 1930s semi?

So what is happening here? Many other countries have mandatory registration schemes for builders, and their citizens are thus given a degree of protection. Maybe that's the reason – because in Britain we are not citizens, we are still her Majesty's subjects, and as such, we do not seem to be entitled to the consumer protection laws enjoyed by other, more modern, states.

Out to Grass (22/2/98)

When the going gets tough, the tough get a bit crafty. The building game has always had its share of scams, most of which involve getting paid but not doing the work. Sometimes, though, when things are really tight, it may be necessary to invent work, so that you get paid for doing things that didn't actually need doing. When builders get talking in the pub, stories of such job creation schemes often get an airing.

My favourite is the ladder-between-two-shops trick which, my sources assure me, was common during the 1930s depression. It goes like this: put the ladder up against the wall between the shops, walk into shop A and say "I've just been cleaning out the gutters next door and I noticed yours are blocked as well – I could do them for a tenner (or other appropriate monetary unit) while I'm up there". Obtain agreement from grateful shop owner, go next door to shop B and repeat. Climb ladder and clean out both gutters, collect money and move on down the street to shops C and D. As scams go, this is only a little bit fraudulent, because the gutters probably needed cleaning out anyway, but the truly inventive might combine this with the old grass seed trick, which involves sprinkling a bit of seed into the cleaned gutters. Some of the seeds lodge in the joints and germinate, so the following year you can return, take the shopkeeper out onto the pavement, and say, "Your gutters need cleaning out again – look, you can see the grass growing in them from down here", which you can. Then you can get commissioned to clean out the gutters before you've even got the ladder up. Crafty. This trick can be repeated on an annual basis.

A modern variant is the waterproof-your-brickwork scam. This involves telling householder A that you are waterproofing the brickwork of house B, and you've got some waterproofer left over – so you can do theirs while you're up there. The waterproofer is, of course, a colourless, odourless, completely safe liquid that will not affect the appearance of the brickwork. Repeat pitch with householder B, climb the ladder and brush the walls of both houses with water carried in an old waterproofer tin.

The leftover carpet scam has been previously described in this column, but continues to thrive. You knock on a door and say you've been carpeting a place up the road and they've ordered too much carpet; you've got enough left to do a whole front room, and you only want a score for it. The trick here is that the "carpet" is the cheapest, thinnest cord stuff with no rubber backing, not really intended for carpeting homes at all; it is generally sold for lining the backs of delivery vans, and is only worth a fiver.

But the cleverest scams are those approved by the mortgage lenders and the surveying profession – those treatments for non-existent rising damp and long-departed woodworm. Like the ladder-between-two-shops trick they gain support from the fact that the neighbours have already had it done, so it must be A Good Thing and, like the old grass seed trick, can be repeated on a regular basis, in many cases every time the property changes hands. With lucrative corporate scams like these around, what need is there to make up your own?

Boring (25/5/97)

If the discussion on site is anything to go by, the water companies are going to have a bit of a job persuading people to save water this summer. The old Water Board could have appealed to the consumer's sense of public duty, and self preservation. Not that we had droughts in those days, of course. Well, we had one once, in 1976, under the last Labour government, but the appointment of my namesake, Dennis Howell, as Minister for Droughts, ensured immediate and continuous flood conditions for the remainder of the decade.

The privatised water companies have managed to get up everyone's nose, though. The feeling on site is that since we are now contributing to the company's profits, it is up to them to make sure the stuff keeps coming out of the taps. Coming on top of the recent desertion of the site's Tory front line troops to the ranks of the Blairistas, this is starting to sound like something of a revolution. That is nothing, however, compared with the positively anarchist sentiments aroused by the plumber's news about boreholes. Apparently, there are people in Essex who are having done with the water companies and all their works and pomps, and are drilling for water in their own back gardens.

Of course, having your own well or borehole is nothing new. Most of the population got their water from boreholes throughout the eighteenth and nineteenth centuries. It was only when filtered water started to be piped in, under pressure, that 'the mains' became a better source of supply. Now, though, the borehole is undergoing something of a resurgence. After the initial expense of having the hole drilled – about three or four grand – you've got free water for life; private domestic users are allowed to extract four thousand gallons per day – no metering, no hose pipe bans. Firms that drill boreholes are going into overdrive – they just can't sink them fast enough. Farmers are major users, of course, and some of them are being a bit naughty, because commercial users are supposed to pay for a licence from the Environment Agency – apparently, drillers are now being asked to do a lot of night work behind hoardings, or even from inside barns.

Environmentally, however, there would seem to be no reason why private borehole usage shouldn't be more advantageous. For a start, you're pumping the water straight from the aquifer to the point of use, avoiding losses due to evaporation and leakage *en route*. You are also going to be as sparing as you can – you've still got to pay for the pumping, usually by submersible electric pump. And the fact is that anyone who has gone to the trouble of sinking a borehole is already aware of the implications of ground water, aquifers and water tables – which is more than can be said of the other 99.9% of the population, who leave the tap running while they clean their teeth and then tut tut at TV news programmes showing rivers running dry.

You don't need an old hippy with a forked willow twig to look for water, by the way; you just consult a hydro-geological map. Much of the southern half of the UK has water-bearing chalk at a reasonable depth, and some of the sandstones in Wales and the North will also yield a good supply. Or you can just consult your local well borer, out of the yellow pages; and yes, the index really does contain the entry 'Boring – see Civil Engineers'.

Plumbers (29/6/97)

You may think you have a problem with your builder's punctuality. Well, if it's any consolation, we builders have our own, more specific version of this problem – why do plumbers never turn up? For plumbers are the Romanies of the building industry – they travel the length and breadth of the land in their brightly painted vans, chock full of mysterious bits and pieces – and nobody ever knows where they are, when they'll turn up next, or where they'll be tomorrow.

Alright, I made up the "brightly painted" bit – most plumbers' vans are white. Ford Escorts usually. But the rest is true; plumbers are the eternal travellers of the building industry. A plumber will drive thirty miles to look at a leak and decide it needs a new washer/valve/pump/diaphragm. But he won't fix it there and then. Oh no. He will drive thirty miles home again, and then make a special trip out the following Tuesday to do the job, after he has driven to the plumbers' merchants to get the special part. So the actual task of fixing the leak takes seven minutes, but there is 150 miles travelling involved which, at 37 pence per mile, comes to ... well, work it out for yourselves. Now you know why it always costs 80 quid when you call the plumber out.

Of course plumbers do have some genuine reasons for not turning up. The "emergency call out" is the most obvious. Burst pipes can wreak havoc in homes – we all know that – and the trusty plumber is duty-bound to respond to a genuine cry for help. Faults with central heating can also be "emergencies". So can blocked drains and overflowing overflows. And emergency call outs command emergency call out fees, and they can result in further work later on. But do plumbers really have to spend so much time driving? Why can't they be more efficient with their time, and carry a complete stock of spare parts? My theory is that plumbers actually prefer driving to working – it's the Romany thing again. And let's face it, if you had to spend your life crawling under sinks or fishing around in toilets, you too might think it better to travel than to arrive. Steve the plumber only ever works in London, but he drives 30 thousand miles a year. Most of it in second gear. He gets through Escort gear boxes like you and I get through dental floss.

But perhaps the most noteworthy thing about plumbers is the ingenuity of their excuses. It will come as no surprise to you to hear that I once called a plumber on his mobile phone, and he answered – I swear this is true – from on board a cross-channel ferry. When I had the temerity to inquire why he was swanning off to the continent instead of connecting up the bidet at 23 Acacia Gardens he said he was "going to get a part for the van". Of all the trades, plumbers have the largest number of plausible excuses at their disposal, and the least compunction about employing them, mercilessly, to give themselves a quiet life.

Over the years I have often thought, if I had my time over again, I would be a plumber. They are the only participants in the building game who get more work as the weather gets worse. I called Steve the plumber last evening, after 72 hours of torrential rain, and he answered the phone with the cry "No, no, yes and maybe". So we know the answer, but what is the question?

Plumbing the Depths (9/11/97)

Never mind European Monetary Union – a unified plumbing system would be a start. A recent survey revealed that what European tourists find most disturbing about Britain is the state of our bathrooms. The lack of adequate showering facilities is a big gripe: "Do the British not wash?" I was asked recently by a German friend. Yes, well, er, maybe we've still got a bit of catching-up to do with regards to that one.

Wash basins are another source of bemusement. Why do we not have mixer taps like the rest of Europe, so you can wash your hands under the running water. Good point – washing your mits at a British basin involves setting the hot tap flowing, soaping up while the water is still running cold, scrubbing as it reaches warm and then rushing to rinse before your skin gets scalded off. Either that, or adopting a unique swinging motion of the upper body, using cupped hands to collect cold and hot water alternately from either side and hoping thus to achieve a comfortable compromise. Not very twenty-first century, is it?

But before we start getting an inferiority complex, it should be noted that not everything across *La Manche* is rosy on the plumbing front either. Some of those Spanish hotels may have showers in the rooms, but have you tried to get a decent flow of hot water out of them? French hole-in-the-ground toilets are a major turn-off for many, and as for those Dutch toilets – you know, the ones with the platforms that allow a close post-operative inspection of the proceedings – well, most of us would rather not know.

It was all started off by the Romans, who introduced piped water right across their Empire, so it may seem odd that plumbing systems across Europe now exhibit such diversity. Our system, it must be said, has developed its own peculiarities – like Australian mammals and American team sports, British plumbing has evolved in isolation, and produced an end product that we know and love, and think of as normal, but which can seem a bit odd to outsiders.

The fact that every British dwelling has its own cold water storage tank, for example, seems unnecessarily complicated, not to mention a potential health hazard, to many mainland Europeans, who are used to using their water direct from the mains. (The correct term is actually cistern, by the way – a tank is a sealed vessel, whilst a cistern is open to atmospheric pressure; so now you know.) All these cisterns provide a total water storage capacity equivalent to several large reservoirs, as well as buffering the effects of pressure fluctuations at times of peak demand. This accustoms the British to a decent flow rate to their baths or showers at any time of the day – the antithesis of the Spanish hotel shower problem. But it also accounts for the lack of mixer taps on our wash basins – we have mains pressure to the cold tap, so you can drink the water, but low pressure cistern water feeding the hot supply – so if you clean your teeth using a mixer tap, you could be swallowing water containing dead pigeons or other unmentionables. I once lived in a flat for two years before I had to investigate a problem with the cistern, and found that the plumber who had installed it had left something behind – a packet of bacon sandwiches. The discovery made me feel quite queasy; give me a good old Dutch toilet any day.

Set the Controls for the Heart of the Sun (21/12/97)

You may have heard that the clocks on 75 per cent of the nation's video recorders are permanently flashing on zero. This statistic is usually quoted to raise a laugh at the technophobia of the wrinklies, but it also points up the shortcomings of the technology; you have to reprogramme the thing when the clocks go back, and also every time you unplug it or if a fuse blows. Most of us just give up. Still, it's a bit of a laugh, eh?

But the manufacturers of central heating systems might not be so amused if they knew how many of their customers were unable to set the timeswitches on their boilers. The Department of the Environment, Transport etc might also take note that its energy-saving advice is falling on incompetent ears; turn the thermostat down? – many people don't know which bit the thermostat *is*, let alone which way is down.

Now, I'm not saying that three out of four people are in this position, but it must be a fair few, and not just the sad old gits, either; I've met plenty of 20 and 30-somethings who haven't worked out how to programme their heating. It is common to find the boiler set permanently "on" and the room thermostat used as an on/off switch, or else for the thermostat to be on "max", and the over-ride trip on the boiler being employed to turn the heating on and off. Both of these methods will warm the place up, of course, but hardly efficiently, and there is no safeguard if the occupants go out and forget to put into effect their version of down, or off.

The new generation of digital controls seems, if anything, to have made things worse. The designers think their control systems are increasingly "user friendly", but the users themselves are getting ever more baffled. The designers are so used to playing with their own gadgets that they can't see things from the point of view of the innumerate general public.

This is often put down to the fact that the technology is designed by men, and is therefore inaccessible to women, but I think there is more to it than that; it also seems to be designed by Lilliputians, who can read instructions and labels that we humans can only detect with electron microscopes. To adjust the humidistat in my bathroom extractor fan, for example, I have to borrow my neighbours' six year-old – he's the only person on the block who can focus on the tiny numbers when he's close enough to turn the miniature dial. And to think that in the old days he'd only have been good for going up chimneys.

On gas-fired radiator systems it is useful to be able to turn the water temperature down – then you can leave the system running when you go away, knowing that the constant low-level heat will stop the pipes freezing and prevent condensation. There is actually a knob that does this – you know, the one that you've always wondered what it's for, or the one hidden away behind the secret panel.

So what's to be done? A major re-education programme is clearly needed; not for the public, but for the people who design appliances for them. Dyson has set a good example with the vacuum cleaner, so now how about central heating that can be programmed by people without electronics degrees, miners' head torches and huge magnifying glasses? There's got to be a market for it.

Smash the Cistern (28/12/97)

It has been estimated that the average Briton flushes the toilet 20 times a day. Who estimates these things? Search me, but they further estimate that 17 of these flushes need only be short, four-and-a-half litre ones; the full nine litre flush is only required three times. You should be able to choose between a short and a long flush if you have a cistern with a little sticker saying something like "short flush – pull and let go; full flush – pull and hold".

But a surprising number of these dual flush cisterns are nothing of the sort, because the installing plumber failed to make one final adjustment – he didn't remove a little piece of rubber from the siphon.

If you think you have a dual flush toilet, but can't tell the difference between holding on and letting go – if you get my drift – then have a look in the top of the cistern. You may have to undo one or two plastic screws to get the lid off. Find the siphon, which is the big plastic tube thingy in the middle, and have a look around the sides of it. There should be a little rubber bung stuck in a hole, below the water level; if you pull it out and look and it, it may even bear the legend "remove this bung for dual flush". Now watch what happens when you pull the lever and let go – the water will fall to the level of the hole, air will be sucked in, and the flush will stop. If you keep the lever held down, the piston blocks off the hole and all the water is siphoned out. Brilliant. So why did the manufacturers bung up the hole in the first place? The reason is that when the cisterns are installed at low level, the short flush is sometimes too feeble, even for those 17-times-a-day situations. So in toilets used by the great British public the building managers usually opt for a constant long flush. In fact, this has been so common that, just when we were getting the hang of them, dual flush cisterns are being phased out; all new cisterns are smaller – seven-and-a-half litres – and give a full flush every time. Since we are supposed to be trying to save water, this does seem like something of a step backwards.

Low level cisterns are also responsible for another problem. Have you ever been in a toilet where the seat will not stay up? This can be very dangerous for men, especially drunken men in unfamiliar toilets. Stop that sniggering; you know what I'm saying. This hazard usually results from the original high level cistern being replaced with a low level one, but without moving the pan forward. So where there used to be room for the lid and seat to be raised past the vertical, and leaned against the flush pipe, now the cistern is in the way. If you have this problem at home then I suggest you get it fixed, at least before your next party; legal claims for that type of personal injury can work out very expensive.

Still, if you do have that particular toilet problem, then at least you will have a greater chance of staying happily married. Because apparently, men leaving toilet seats up is one of the most frequently-cited complaints in divorce proceedings. Who estimated that? Search me, but all the women I've mentioned it to agree that it *must* be true.

Pyramid Selling (18/5/97)

The shock events of May 1st are still reverberating around the building industry. Nobody has been able to talk much about anything else. Foreman, electrician, bricklayer, carpenter – one topic of conversation has dominated on site – is the pyramid-shaped tea bag really an improvement? The depth of debate has been impressive, on a site not noted as a hotbed of radical thought, so there is clearly something about tea that has stirred (sorry) the proletarian thought train.

It was May Day when the triangular box of free samples appeared on the doorstep of the job. Everyone in the country has had one, apparently; Brooke Bond have a better distribution system than the Liberal Democrats. The views expressed on the new product have largely reflected trade demarcations – the plumber is sceptical about the manufacturers' water circulation claims, while the carpenter appreciates the design, which always leaves a corner sticking out of the cup to aid removal (there is never a teaspoon on site or, if there is, it has been stuck, wet, into the sugar bag); this is acknowledged as giving the pyramid bag an advantage over Tetley's round tea bag, which, presumably, is the competition. The labourer pointed out that the pyramid is not actually a pyramid but a tetrahedron. This caused a moment or two of reflection, but I pointed out that the labourer is not actually a labourer but a sculptor, so what would he know about, er, shapes.

The degree of attention given to the debate (and I mean serious concentrated attention – we're talking *blind tasting tests* here) is an indication of the importance tea drinking plays in the life of the building worker. Tea is a stimulant and its consumption is symbolic and ritualistic. Not quite on the level of your Japanese Tea Ceremony, granted, but an important ritual nonetheless.

When you're working in someone's house, the punter

sometimes seems to think you spend too long drinking tea, and not enough time working. This is very rarely the case, although what can happen is that different trades may be partaking of refreshment at different times. This can give the impression that there is always a tea break going on; there might be, but not everyone is taking part in it. The wet trades, and plasterers especially, have their routines dictated by the setting times of the materials, and will have their breaks accordingly.

The builders' tea ceremony has another manifestation when it is played out in the cafe. Builders go to the cafe for breakfast at ten o'clock. All of them. If there are five jobs on the go in the vicinity of a greasy spoon cafe, then the workers from all five sites will be there at ten. Any talk of staggered visiting hours or flexi-time is out of the question. So you get thirty blokes queuing up at ten, and at half past the place is empty again. That's part of the ritual. Another part goes like this: suppose there are four of you from your site; you all order separately at the counter and pay for your own breakfast, but the first one up gets the teas in for everybody, as though it's a round of drinks in the pub. Then, half way through breakfast, the next one gets another round in. And so on. If you try and buck the trend, by buying yourself, say, a cappuccino, you can get yourself a reputation as a pinko vegetarian agitator. The sort who remembers the real significance of May Day, for example.

Drink (8/6/97)

Drink has been the cause of many a dispute between builder and client over the years. I don't mean the consequences of inebriation, although God knows, there's enough of that about. Building is thirsty work, and the partaking of cold beverages is common amongst its practitioners. No, I mean the use of the word 'drink' as a euphemism for a non-taxable gratuity.

All professions have their slang words for a bit of cash on the side: in football it's a 'bung'; in business, a 'perk'; in Tory politics, a 'weekend for two in the Paris Ritz'. In legal terms, of course, these inducements all come under the general term 'bribes', but that's another matter. When dealing with builders, you will often hear the expression "I'll do it for a drink", and herein lies the source of confusion. What, exactly, is a drink? Well, it is probably easier to say what it is not. For example, one woman I know inveigled next door's builders into carrying half a ton of putrefying garden waste out through the house and into their guvnor's skip 'for a drink', and seriously thought they would be pleased by her offer of a cup of tea. She quickly found that tea, in this context, does not constitute a drink. Nor does a can of Sainsbury's lager out of the fridge. In fact, a whole crate of lager will not do. Nor, for that matter, will a hogshead of the finest Port, or a case of 1961 Pichon Longueville. For what is needed is cash. Of the folding variety.

What can be even more confusing for the middle classes is that the size of the 'drink' does not necessarily relate to the amount needed to buy a round of drinks in the pub. As far as anyone can tell, there are no hard and fast rules about the exact sum involved, but if its purchasing power was to be related in any way to actual alcohol consumption, it could well be enough to render the recipient unconscious. In the East End of London a drink can be £10, £20 or, taking inflationary pressures into account, £30. In the West End, a drink has been known to be £50. Anything above this takes us into the higher bracket of a 'good drink', which can be up to £100, and then a 'big drink', which is £100 to £500. Readers are advised to avoid deals where big drinks are mentioned, as the sums involved generally indicate at least tangential exposure to some kind of criminal activity.

If there is any degree of confusion or ambiguity about the sum involved, the answer, as always, is to ask. If, in the course of negotiations, a builder says 'Give me a drink, then', say 'How much is a drink?' It's alright to haggle – nobody will be offended.

It is much better to admit ignorance from the off than to get the job done and for the builder then to think you are tight, or worse, scheming.

Note, also, that a drink is completely separate from slang terms such as a score, a pony, a nifty, a ton and a monkey, indicating £20, £25, £50, £100 and £500 respectively. Again, be careful negotiating when expressions like this are used – people who make a habit of using prole slang when dealing with middle class punters are quite likely to be from privileged backgrounds themselves. They talk this way to give themselves a bit of street cred, and may not actually be sure what the terms mean. Builders like this, in fact, may well be talked into doing you a favour in return for a cup of tea. Earl Grey, of course.

Slang (15/6/97)

There has been a remarkable response to last week's column about drink – or rather to the bit about monetary units used in negotiating deals with builders. It seems that slang terms for cash are a recurring source of misunderstanding, especially between working-class builders and middle-class punters. Obviously, when Karl Marx was sat in the beautiful central reading room of the British Library, composing his ideas for *Das Kapital*, this was the chapter he didn't get around to writing. Or perhaps he did, and his editor decided to cut it out – some things never change.

Anyway, here is Marx's missing chapter, entitled "Building Economics – or how to decipher what your builder means when he says he'll do your drains for a one-er".

Starting with last week's list of cash sums, the score and the ton should have been self-explanatory, at least to anyone who was at school before 1979. The nifty fifty is clearly cockney rhyming slang. It was the pony and the monkey which generated most attention – why do they mean what they mean? Well, the £25 pony is derived, of course, from Mammoth, Britain's largest ever Shire Horse, which was owned by Mr Thomas Cleaver of Toddington Mill, Beds, and which was measured in 1846, allegedly, at 25 hands. This clearly created a bit of a stir in the press at the time and, since '25 hands' sounds like '25 pounds' (well, it does if you say it an exaggerated hollywood-style cockney accent) it came into general use for that sum.

The £500 monkey derives from Bukhama, Britain's largest gorilla, who lived in Dudley Zoo from 1860 to 1869, and weighed – yes, you've guessed it – 500 pounds. So there you go. Many thanks to Bethnal Green Eddie, carpenter and roofer of this parish, for research on this important topic, for, although the terms are in common use, not many people, apart from Independent on Sunday readers, know, or care about, their origin.

Another cash sum you might hear mentioned includes a one-er, which is generally £100, but which can sometimes be short-hand for £1000. More usual terms for £1000 are a grand, a long'un, and a k (pronounced "kay" – do not confuse with a ki, pronounced "key", which is used, allegedly, in drug deals to denote a kilogram).

Car dealers, by the way, have their own monetary system, and deal in hundreds. So your old Volvo, which has a book price of £4200, will be worth "42 hundred", or simply "42", with or without its antique dealer's roof rack. Roll on European Monetary Union, I say.

But what other slang words would it be useful to know in order to steal a march on your builder? To a certain extent all trade terms are slang, or jargon, traditionally used to exclude outsiders from the conversation. There is a school of social anthropology which defines the old craft apprenticeships as initiation rites, during which the (illiterate) trainees were taught the secret words which described parts of buildings. This process sometimes reached absurd extremes, as with stone masonry, which evolved into the even greater absurdity of freemasonry. But all the trades have their own words for things, including themselves. Bricklayers are called trowels – hence newspaper adverts for brickies specify that "fast, clean trowels only need apply". Brickies' labourers are called hods. Plasterers are known as spreads, carpenters as chippies, and electricians are sparks. Plumbers are called all sorts of things, mainly because they never turn up when they're supposed to, and when they do, they then have to go away to fetch a special part from a special place in Dagenham, which takes another three days.

Stoned Masons (14/12/97)

In case you were wondering about this column's position on the cannabis campaign, I am pleased to be able to report that drug-taking in the building industry is at an all-time high. For many years now, cannabis has been the drug of choice for the manual trades. There should be no surprise about this – most building workers are aged 16 to 35, and their drug-taking habits will be the same as any other group of their generation – students, footballers, social workers. Howard Marks reckons the British consume around three tons of cannabis every day, and it stands to reason that one million construction workers must account for a fair bit of that.

An added incentive for building workers to take drugs has been the crackdown on lunchtime drinking, which is clearly a good thing; no-one wants people charging around the scaffolding after three pints of lager. But, as anthropologists have discovered, young men always want to get out of their crusts on something, so all the usual recreational drugs can be found on building sites.

Brickies and hod-carriers can commonly be seen smoking hash in little roll-ups. The tobacco/drug ratio is usually about 99 to one, so there is no negative effect on productivity; in fact, the net result probably favours the employer, because where a brickie would formerly have savoured a leisurely fag under the eyes of the foreman, with a spliff he is far more furtive – one puff and straight back to work – smoking? me? of course not. It's the back-of-the-bikesheds scenario all over again; when it's legalised we'll miss all of that.

Painters, too, are fond of the weed, and with such a monotonous job, who can blame them. Or maybe they see themselves as creative types; after all, there is an honourable history of painters taking mind-expanding drugs – Van Gogh saw those sunflowers in a different light after an afternoon on the Absinthe, didn't he – or was it lead poisoning from licking his paint brushes?

Some labourers take amphetamines, and there are many others who don't, but probably should. The problem with speed, though, is that it can turn them into gibbering idiots; they turn up with the bricks at double quick time, but then stand there yakking on about music or football and forget to go back for the next load.

Plasterers also favour stimulants rather than hallucinogens; the nature of their work demands quick bursts of activity before the plaster starts to set; so speed and cocaine are popular with plastering gangs. Some of the highest earning spreads use speed *and* cocaine, but I've never been quite sure whether it's the drugs that make them work fast, or whether they have to work fast to earn the money to pay for the drugs.

Ecstasy is the big drug at the moment, and there are clearly lots of people walking around on site smiling far too much. It is debatable whether they are taking E in order to further their appreciation of shovelling concrete, however – most of them look, and smell, as if they have come to work straight from last night's rave, which is often the case. A building contractor mate of mine, who used to sack labourers for turning up late for work, has now taken to sacking the ones who arrive too early. He says he'd sooner have guys with hangovers than ravers still tripping. So who says the construction industry is lax about health and safety?

Surveys (11/5/97)

The announcement of a multi-million pound deficit in the education budget will have come as no surprise to construction lecturers. Training and education in the construction industry is at an all-time low. On-the-job training of bricklayers, carpenters and other trades has all but disappeared, replaced with compulsory six week courses for the unemployed. Do you wonder why your new home has been constructed so badly? It was built as part of someone's punishment.

The education of construction professionals such as architects and building surveyors has similarly been in a nose dive. Time was when the seven year architecture diploma included hands-on experience in plastering, painting and bricklaying, but the current three year degree is theory only; the nearest students get to building experience these days is making models out of chicken wire and toilet rolls. The result is that newly qualified construction professionals are being sent out into the real world handicapped not just by the usual deficiencies in literacy and numeracy, but without much knowledge of buildings either.

But most people are still under the impression that when they get a chartered surveyor to give their new house the once-over, they will be getting some kind of definitive expert view of the building by an experienced professional. Not so. What you are getting, more often than not, is someone who got an A-level in Geography, spent three years in the classroom at a 'New University', and then got a job in a surveying practice. There, they will have been taken under the wing of a slightly older surveyor, who probably advised them to "forget everything they learned [sic] at college", and took them out to do mortgage valuation surveys. These entail filling in the blank spaces on a printed form, such as "State whether main water, drainage, electricity and gas are connected"; a typical reply to which is, "All mains services appear to be connected but have not been tested". You could do better yourself.

A clue to the limited nature of surveyors' investigations can be had from the clothes they wear to work. Most surveyors turn up in their best suits, hardly well equipped for climbing up into the loft or having a poke round in the gutters. They won't even want to get down on one knee for fear of dirtying their trousers, which rules out looking at the drains or even lifting the edge of a carpet. In fact the standard home buyers' report includes the stock phrase, "Furniture, wall hangings, floor coverings, insulation material and stored goods have not been moved". So if you are selling a house and you don't want the surveyor to notice some particularly dodgy detail, just hide it with a few tea chests or a bit of carpet.

Even when they do try to 'investigate' a bit deeper surveyors manage to give the impression of being totally ignorant. In a study by South Bank University, for example, 93% of surveyors questioned did not know how to use a moisture meter correctly to diagnose dampness problems in walls. The result is that, rather than risk making mistakes and laying themselves open to future compensation claims, surveyors always recommend "further investigation" by others of tricky subjects like dampness. Their reports give *carte blanche* to cowboy builders to come in with estimates for thousands of pounds worth of unnecessary work, all sanctioned by the surveyors and, therefore, by the mortgage lenders.

But why get a survey done at all if it is so inadequate? The answer lies in the Building Societies Act of 1986, which requires a written valuation report to be obtained on the occasion of each advance. Maybe someone in the new administration should take a look at this important consumer issue. After all, as Adam Smith pointed out, all professions are a conspiracy against the public.

The Surveys that Reveal Nothing (15/3/98)

The proposed scrapping of mortgage valuation surveys sounds like bad news for surveyors but good news for home buyers. The need for an independent valuation when lending against a property was enshrined by act of parliament – the Building Societies Act, 1986. But this was back in the days when building societies were mutual societies, owned by their lenders and borrowers – now most of them have either become banks or been taken over by banks, and they are no longer bound by the Act; they can lend money to whoever they like, whenever they like. So if you want to buy a home, fine – it doesn't really matter what the place is worth; as long as you are in employment, and with no black marks on your credit record, then most mortgage lenders will advance you two or three times your annual salary. The more they lend, the more they get back in interest. The idea that the property had to be redeemable in case you defaulted was always a bit of a red herring, because even in the depths of recession and negative equity most people kept paying the mortgage – on average, fewer than five per cent of mortgaged homes ever get repossessed. So the massed ranks of newly-privatised mortgage lenders have calculated that they can risk losing out on a few dodgy mortgage deals and still make a profit for their shareholders – and of course if they can lend money over the phone, without the pesky business of getting a surveyor to look at the property first, it will give them a distinct marketing advantage over those building societies still hanging on to mutual status. And that, children, is what capitalism is all about.

As a horny-handed son of toil, I suppose I should be wary about all this free-market manoeuvring, but, in truth, I find it hard to lament the passing of the mortgage valuation survey. The whole exercise is an expensive bit of ritual where a bloke in a suit glances over the property, makes a few banal observations, and then gives you a shopping list of other specialists – to take a closer look at your drains, electrics, damp-proof course, woodworm holes and wall ties. These "specialists", who know that your getting a mortgage hinges on them giving you a realistic-sounding estimate for some sort of work, are only too happy to oblige. Result? – a thousand quid's-worth of estimates, a thousand quid retained by the lender, and a metaphorical noose tightening around your neck to persuade you to agree to everything.

The Royal Institution of Chartered Surveyors say they were never keen on mortgage valuations anyway; they always recommend shelling out for the more expensive "homebuyers' survey and valuation". This might sound like tempting advice, but, apart from getting ten pages of banalities instead of one, the end result is almost identical – the guy still turns up dressed in his best suit; he won't look under carpets, behind wardrobes or anywhere spiders might be hiding; and he still recommends that everything gets checked by other "specialists" in case any of his opinions might get him into trouble later.

Architects (10/8/97)

If you want to get building work done properly, you are supposed to first engage an architect to produce a set of drawings. You may hear these referred to as *plans* but really the plan is only the drawing showing the horizontal lay-out – the bird's eye view; you will also need *elevations* – the front, back and side pictures of the building – and *sections*, which show the cut-away details. A competent architect will also be able to provide you with a *bill of quantities*, listing all the activities to be carried out and the materials to be used. If you then ask three builders to tender for the work, based upon the same drawings and bill of quantities, you will be sure that the three prices you get are all for the same end product. The architect should also be able to negotiate with the builders on your behalf, produce a *schedule of works* – which spells out in idiot-proof terms the exact sequence of operations – and supervise the construction work.

This is the traditional way. Generations of architects have carried out this valuable service, designing and supervising buildings from the humblest of back additions to the grandest of stately homes. Architects used to cut their teeth on this kind of work, and most went on to pursue it for a living.

But now, be warned, there is increasing fragmentation in the architecture game, and many of the new generation think their role is to be the next Richard Rogers, designing unusual buildings different from anything built before, rather than making a good job of your new kitchen extension.

Remember the Monty Python sketch where architect John Cleese wants to equip the new Town Hall with rotating knives, because he usually designs slaughter houses? This is hilarious because it is so nearly true. Architects develop specialisms, and someone who is a whizz at out-of-town shopping malls may not have the touch required for alterations to a Regency terrace. You can see examples of this insensitivity wherever you look – old period houses corrupted with new details straight off the pages of the latest Italian design mags – by architects who want to build monuments to themselves rather than work sympathetically with existing buildings.

Others are just plain ignorant. On a recent job, the architect had decided the new back addition was to be built in reclaimed bricks to match those in the main house, and had specified second-hand yellow London stocks. Unfortunately, the original house had not been built with yellow stocks at all, but with *gaults*, creamy-white bricks fired from gault clay. An easy mistake for a lay person to make, you might think; but shouldn't an architect be able to do better?

I heard this week of another architect, who did not understand that yard gulleys – the ground-level inlets which direct surface water away to the drains – should always contain water. A yard gulley has a "trap", or U-bend full of water – just like a toilet bowl – to stop smells coming up from the sewers. This architect spotted the water lying in the trap of a new gulley and called the builder back, complaining that the new drainage system was blocked. People like this are supposed to be experts, charging clients hefty fees for the benefits of their construction skill and experience, but all they seem to do is bring the rest of their august profession into disrepute. Still, if we continue to train architects by getting them to make models out of plasticine and empty bog rolls, what else should we expect?

Designing for Dummies (19/10/97)

The last government's prediction that 4.4 million new homes need to be built by 2016 has raised predictable protests. Even if half of them were built on "brownfield" sites in towns, the scale of development in the countryside would still be huge. Up to 120 square miles of land would be needed, and many villages would have their characters irredeemably spoiled.

The counter argument is that it is time more people lived out of town, and building homes in rural areas would only be redressing the balance to that of the last century, before the great drift to the cities began.

Whatever the arguments against despoiling the green belt and increasing road traffic, the major objection to more new homes in the countryside must be simply how inappropriate modern houses look in a rural setting. Most villages now have at least one area which could easily be mistaken for any suburb of any city – a stretch of road with a row of identical brick boxes. From Norfolk to Northumbria, the style and materials are the same – sand-faced red bricks, concrete roof tiles, double-glazed casement windows and garages with up-and-over steel doors – not a hint of local character or distinctiveness anywhere.

But it doesn't have to be like this. I recently had the privilege of attending a talk by David Oliver, District Architect of the West Dorset District Council. Mr Oliver's patch includes Poundbury, the Prince of Wales's pet project; some of the principles being applied there, and in other parts of West Dorset, should be a lesson for Town Planners everywhere. Mr Oliver and his team encourage the development of *real* villages, with shops, pubs, and each house different from the next.

Suburban developments on the edge of a village are discouraged, as residents have to use their cars to get anywhere, they are prime sites for burglary and, apparently, nobody knows their neighbours. And one of the planning dreams of such developments, that they are safe for children to play in, is not even true – with the houses set back from the road and clear lines of sight for drivers, they actually encourage speeding.

Mr Oliver says the way to slow traffic is to actually build houses right up to the edge of the road, especially on bends; with a blind corner every 50 metres even the most reckless boy racer will find it hard to get over 20 mph; so no need for speed bumps or other artificial traffic calming measures. Certainly recent photos of Poundbury show people walking, cycling and stopping for a chat in the high street, with car drivers inching their way carefully around them; HGV drivers, presumably, give the place a wide berth.

Another advantage of building close up to the road is that passers-by can't look in the upstairs windows, whilst modern houses set back from the road have to have net curtains in the bedrooms. Mr Oliver also disapproves of the ceiling and window dimensions of modern houses – he says they are too high – and he likes to see tradesmen playing their part in the design process; on one site the bricklayers were asked to design the chimneys, based upon their observations of traditional buildings in the area; needless to say their pride in their work quickly extended to the rest of the building.

So it may not be housing people in the countryside that is the problem, but rather the type of housing. Local authority planning departments would do well to invite David Oliver to address them, and to take note of what he says.

Through the Roof (15/2/98)

I don't set out to have a go at architects; I really don't. But sometimes I hear tales about such staggering incompetence that I just have to pass them on, as a warning to others.

So I recently heard about this couple who have bought an old stable in the country, to convert into their dream retirement home, and they've hired an architect – *highly recommended by friends* – where have we heard that one before? – and the architect's plans have included a number of large, expensive, Swedish roof windows. Now, roof windows are a bit contentious at the best of times; they let a lot of light in, and are often used to turn dingy roof spaces into sun-drenched loft conversions. But conservationists don't like them, because you have to lose a chunk of your original roof tiles to insert this very obvious Swedish-look double glazed panel. And roof windows can also be responsible for solar glare, bouncing the sun's rays into the eyes of innocent passing motorists – in fact some local authorities have banned them for this very reason. In general, though, roof windows, unlike dormer windows, can be put into old buildings without planning permission, and architects and interior designers love them because of the way they let in the light.

Whatever, the old stable block was set to be given the all-over Swedish look with a rash of huge roof windows. The builder duly ordered them and they were delivered to site. Then the trouble started. The builder, a conscientious sort, could not fail to notice that several of the roof windows were so big that they would span across the purlins – the big horizontal timbers which support the rafters – and so the windows could not be opened. Being conscientious, he pointed this out to the architect, whose response was what led to this story. Because the architect, this supposedly learned man, this expert in the ways of all building things, asked if the purlins could not be removed. "Not without the roof falling in, they can't", replied the builder. And so it came to pass that the purlins remained in place, and the expensive Swedish windows were installed on top of them, and cannot now be opened. So they cannot be cleaned from the inside, and in the summer the solar gain through their huge glazed surfaces will heat the place up to sauna temperature whilst they remain firmly shut.

And the punters have *paid* for this debacle. They have paid good money to a man who professes to be a building expert but who, it transpires, does not know the first thing about how roofs are put together. And that, dear reader, is why this column has had to return again to the question of architects. Last week I discussed the problem of trying to find a decent builder; but what about a competent architect? Does their professional association monitor their behaviour? Do they have to submit a selection of their work for judgement by their peers? Of course not; once qualified, architects are free to practice unobserved for the rest of their working lives, and the punters, by and large, have to make do with their cock-ups.

So, all you architects who write in and tell me I don't know what I'm talking about, and ask what qualifies me to pass judgement – just think for a minute – are you sure you could pass the purlin test?

The Fool who Designs Good Buildings (8/3/98)

I had a nice surprise last week; I got a letter, with a French postmark, from that Léon Krier – the architect who worked with the Prince of Wales on Poundbury, the new village development in Dorset. Now, you will understand that my postbag in the past few weeks has contained quite a few letters, most of them of the irate-architect-from-Ongar type, telling me off for daring to question architects' divine right to bugger the place up for the rest of us. So when I opened the envelope and saw that the boy Krier had taken the trouble to write to me, in his own hand, I naturally feared the worst. I need not have worried; turns out he's read my views on Poundbury, and I'm the only person to have written anything complimentary about the place in any British newspaper for the past five years; so he'd be very honoured if I'd attend his book launch at The Prince of Wales's Institute of Architecture in Regent's Park – or Camden Town as we call it down here.

Before I proceed I must declare an interest – well, two interests actually. The first is that I think that most ordinary people feel more comfortable with classical architecture than with modernist glass-and-concrete boxes; and the second is that when I arrived at The Prince of Wales's Institute I found there was no beer, so I was forced to quaff huge quantities of white wine, my glass being constantly refilled by a team of hovering waiters. I'm not complaining for one minute, but I thought I'd better mention it. I ended up chatting to a very nice man who said he'd designed Milton Keynes once but he now mostly does racecourses.

Anyway, the boy Krier has been a bit demonised in this country. I first came across him a few years ago when I saw his design for a building for New College, Oxford University – it had solid brick walls and stepped brick footings with no foundations – just like every other building constructed on the site for the past thousand years. Naturally, the college's governing body rejected the plan, even though engineers' calculations showed that it was a perfectly sound design, and would conform to all the requirements of the building regulations. Clearly Krier thinks new buildings should fit in with existing ones, and provide pleasant spaces for people to live and work in, rather than be monuments to those who designed them. In the eyes of the modernists this apparently makes him a dangerous, demented radical. Still, as the man from Ongar said, what do I know about it?

Wallpaper Job

More on how to choose a builder. There seems to be a rapid growth of schemes, such as Barclaycard Home Assist and HSA (Hospital Savings Association) Home Emergency Care, offering to put you in touch with "reliable tradesmen". Exactly how qualified and experienced these tradesmen are is not made clear in the brochures, and obviously I would not criticise these schemes without knowing more about them, but a reader writes in from Norwich about a builder recommended by the AA's Home Moving Service; he's been waiting six months and the bloke still hasn't started the job. Do these schemes really provide a service to the public, or are they just another marketing tool for the organisations concerned? British consumers deserve a proper government-administered builders' registration scheme ... even that bloke who wallpapered the Lord Chancellor's apartment could get on it.

Anything for a Lath (12/10/97)

Bethnal Green Eddie is not a happy man. He has put himself out to do someone a favour, and then been told he has done the job wrong.

The job in question was a lath-and-plaster ceiling, cracked and sagging, but still worth trying to save, not least for the intricately moulded Victorian cornicing still in place around the edges. Your average builder or plasterer would rip the whole lot down, tack up a few sheets of plasterboard, and skim them with a pink gypsum finish coat. If you wanted to keep the cornicing it would have to be copied, at great expense, in new fibrous plaster or replaced by some tacky modern imitation. The new plasterboard ceiling would look dead flat, changing the period feel, and acoustics, of the room, and in time would crack along the joints of the boards – and yet another little piece of our dwindling building heritage would be lost forever.

But Eddie, being sympathetic to old buildings, gave up his weekend to carefully remove the damaged sections of plaster, clean and re-nail the riven chestnut laths, and apply a fresh coat of lime plaster. It was a fiddly, time-consuming but ultimately rewarding job, a simple but worthwhile bit of building conservation in a world of ripping-out and throwing-away. The owner didn't know how lucky he was – you try getting a specialist conservation plasterer to come and do your ceiling; you'll have to take out a second mortgage just to get one round to look at it; they're all working down at Windsor Castle, being photographed for fancy interiors magazines.

So when, after the weekend, Eddie got a call from the owner of the new ceiling, he thought it would mean, if not a crate of bubbly, then at least a few words of thanks. The last thing he was expecting was to be bawled out for ruining the house and endangering the lives of everyone in it. Seems the punter had gone in to work with the story of his lath-and-plaster ceiling, and been told by his mates that you aren't allowed to have them any more, that they're not up to modern fire safety standards, and that it would all have to come down again and be replaced – with plasterboard.

Two questions here: why do people always believe what their mates at work tell them, and whence came the idea that traditional building materials, tried and tested over hundreds of years, should suddenly become unsafe? I can't answer the first one; office people seem to spend most of their time at work moaning about their colleagues – who they think are inefficient, misguided or just plain ignorant – until it comes to advice about building, when the colleagues suddenly become fascinating purveyors of the latest expert knowledge.

The answer to the second question lies, I believe, with a misunderstanding of the Building Regulations, the DoE guidelines which lay down minimum standards for new building work. Now, 99.9% of the population have never clapped eyes on the Building Regs. But they have heard reference to them, usually accompanied by a sucking through the teeth noise, when some cowboy builder has been trying to cover up his lack of craft skills by using some ghastly new gadget or material: "You don't want this old rubbish, you want to get rid of that and put up some plasterboard – it's the Building Regulations innit?" For once, the manufacturers are not to blame; they don't have to tell you to tear down your Victorian ceilings; they've got your mates at work to do it for them.

In the Limelight (2/11/97)

Let's be clear about this – lime-and-hair plaster is to modern gypsum plaster what your old granny's Madeira cake is to an instant sponge cake mix. The one is made from carefully selected local ingredients, requires skill and patience to perfect, and turns out slightly different every time, which adds to its character. The other is made by opening a packet and adding water – within the hour you've got your functional but bland result, always the same whatever the season and whichever part of the country you are in.

Does this matter? Well, it does if you like real cakes and real buildings. The manufacturers of instant cake mixes, like the makers of instant plaster mixes, will doubtless say they are only supplying what their customers want. Nothing wrong with that, but the danger is that the customers want these products only because they have been brought up with them; they often don't realise there is another way – a way which doesn't involve buying a packet with the instructions on.

So when a young plasterer – in his teens or twenties say – is working in an old building with a patch of damaged plaster on the wall, the only material he knows how to use is gypsum plaster. So he mixes it up and spreads it over the offending area; bosh bosh, loadsamoney, as we all used to say. But the gypsum plaster behaves differently from the lime; it is harder and less flexible; so soon a crack will show up where the two materials meet. And if the plasterer makes the common mistake of using gypsum plaster on the inside of an external brick wall, something else will happen – after a while the plaster will get damp and the wallpaper or paint will start to discolour. This is because gypsum plasters dissolve when they get wet. Experienced plasterers know this, so they use sand and cement render on external walls; this stuff certainly won't dissolve, but it doesn't allow the wall to breathe either, and so can create other kinds of dampness problems.

Now, lime is one of the oldest building materials; it has been used successfully for thousands of years, and only in the last thirty years or so have we abandoned it. Unfortunately, it only takes one generation for knowledge to be lost; there are still a few plasterers in their sixties who were taught to use lime as apprentices, but few of them are passing the skills on. This is hardly surprising when kids are now told that the skill they most need is to be able to use the internet. All very useful, I'm sure, but you'll never get a computer to plaster your ceiling.

So, if you are getting some plastering done on an old building, try getting your plasterer to do it in lime. Purists insist on using real slaked lime, but bagged hydrated lime from the builders' merchants will give a reasonable result, knocked up with washed plastering sand – cover it up and leave it to stand for three days before using. The only tricky bit is getting the hair, but you can order this by phone from IJP Building Conservation (0118 969 6949). They do horse, goat and cow hair for £10 per kilo, and a kilo of hair will do about half a tonne of plaster. Your plasterer will almost certainly want to add cement to the mix, because he will have been told that lime on its own won't work. You will just have to be firm here – explain that if lime worked for the Romans then it will work for him too.

Pointing (11/1/98)

It's rude to point, and it's usually bad for buildings too. Pointing is the name given to the tooled pattern of mortar between the bricks, so called because it used to be shaped with the point of the trowel. It still is, sometimes, or other tools can be used to give different shapes; for example, old galvanised steel bucket handles are run along the wet mortar to form a concave joint called ..... well, a bucket handle joint, funnily enough. (Let's face it, we bricklayers are too honest for our own good; a carpenter would call it something esoteric like nogging or sprocketing, and make it sound much more difficult and clever).

Anyway, repointing is the act of hacking out the old pointing and sticking some new stuff in. It hardly ever needs doing, but architects and surveyors like to say it does – well, they have to say something to justify their fees, don't they? Pointing rarely needs replacing because it should be a *sacrificial* material. That is, it is supposed to be softer and more porous than the bricks, and so allow thermal and moisture movement to take place without the bricks themselves being damaged. After many years – maybe 50 or 100 – the pointing will have weathered back, and may need some attention, but unless the wear is extreme, or you can see daylight between the bricks, it is usually better left alone.

Conservation pointing is a very skilled job, and the aim is to restore the integrity of a wall but leave it looking as though you haven't touched it. This is too much for some builders, who think repointing should make an 18th-century wall looking as though it was put up last week; they like to rake out the soft old lime mortar and force nice thick stripes of hard sand and cement into the joints. The wall will look as if it has been re-drawn using a blunt pencil, and will immediately start to suffer problems. For one thing the new sand and cement will be too hard, so any movement will result in the bricks cracking or, if you're lucky, in the new pointing being squeezed out. The other problem is that sand and cement is impermeable to moisture, so wetting and drying of the wall has to take place through the bricks themselves; this results in efflorescence (salt crystallisation), moss growth and frost damage. If the wall is in an exposed position, within a few years the faces of the bricks will have blown off, leaving ridges of new pointing standing proud between them. Cement pointing has probably destroyed more Victorian brickwork than the Luftwaffe.

But don't take my word for it; ask the people who repointed Hadrian's Wall. The bit of Hadrian's Wall that you can see today is the bottom half; it survived for 2000 years because it had been buried by drifting earth. Then it was excavated in the 1920s, and the restorers decided to repoint it with a nice rich mix of sand and cement; within a few years the stones had started to crumble. So in 1986 English Heritage started a research project to find the most suitable mortar for repairing the wall; they have now found the best one to be a mix of lime, sand and crushed brick, and the worst to be any mortar containing cement. Oh well, as Hadrian himself might have said, *Praestat Sero Quam Nunquam.*

The Doors of Perception (30/11/97)

Were you born in a barn? No? Good – then shut the bloody door. Five top reasons for closing doors:

One – heat. Heat is a precious commodity. Internal doors keep it where it is needed. If you leave the doors open the heat will go upwards and outwards. It is worth remembering that *central* heating does not in itself warm the whole house; the term derives from the fact that one central heat source (the boiler or heat exchanger) provides heat which is *distributed* to the rest of the house, via radiators, hot air ducts, or whatever. Once there it ends up as warm air, which has to be kept in place long enough to give up its heat to the structure and fabric of the room; closed doors are vital for the success of the whole operation. If the internal doors are left open the upstairs rooms will get most of the heat, and the downstairs will stay cold, which may lead to ...

Two – condensation. Inside air always contains more moisture than outside air. The extra moisture is produced by people – breathing, sweating, washing, cooking. Keeping the doors shut keeps the moisture where it is produced; it should be allowed to escape only to the outside, by opening the windows. If you leave the doors to the "wet" rooms open then you will get condensation on cold surfaces all around the house, especially in those cold corners downstairs. Is there mildew on your old leather jacket when you get it out of the wardrobe? Then try closing the bathroom door after your shower.

Three – fire. Even an ordinary timber panelled door can keep a fire at bay for hours. It stops flames and smoke from spreading and, more importantly, stifles the fire by limiting the air supply. Open the door and – whoosh – a fire can engulf the rest of the house in minutes. Modern doors are fire-rated, which refers to the time they are designed to contain a blazing fire – half-hour, one-hour etc. Old period doors can have their fire rating increased by attaching fire-resistant boarding on one side; this is preferable to replacing them with featureless new fire doors when converting houses into flats.

By the way, fire doors have to be self-closing; in public buildings you often see them propped open ... with fire extinguishers (well, there's always one handy). People that do this should be sent to prison.

Four – noise. Closed doors, and windows, are surprisingly effective at keeping sounds within rooms. People that like playing their stereos very loud know this, so they often open all the doors and windows so as to share their listening pleasure with everybody else. Thoughtful of them.

Closing your own internal doors can even help deaden noise from outside and from the neighbours. If the doors are open, the sound can move around, by reflection, reverberation and resonance, and come out in different places, just like with the openings in a loudspeaker cabinet. Closing the doors divides the building up into separate compartments and reduces these effects.

Five – privacy. Until recently, doors opened in towards the centre of the room, so someone standing at the half-opened door had a restricted view into the room. Now, concepts of privacy and personal space have changed, and doors are generally hinged to open the other way, back against the end wall, offering an uninterrupted view. Funny, that.

Six – was there a six? Oh yes, as my old man used to say, because I bloody say so.

Hubble Bubble (28/9/97)

The British like to affect a casual indifference to the buildings in which they live, work and are entertained. This attitude enables them to abdicate responsibility for the buildings' care and defer to a small group known as "builders". As an example, take the common problem of condensation. If people cared for their homes they would make sure the water vapour produced by cooking, showering or washing clothes was directed to the outside of the building rather than allowed to circulate inside, looking for suitable cold surfaces to condense on. Every building is equipped with a simple mechanism for achieving this objective – it is called opening the windows. When the "wet" rooms – kitchen, bathroom & utility room – are being used, the windows should be open and the internal doors to the rest of the house should be closed. But many people will not do this; they prefer to keep their bathroom and kitchen windows closed and, if the rooms get a bit steamy, will even open the internal doors to allow the fog to disperse. The result is that water vapour finds its way into rooms and cupboards far away from the source and condenses out onto cooler surfaces. This usually initiates black mould growth on walls and ceilings and green mildew on shoes and fabrics – leather jackets and handbags hanging in built-in wardrobes in the bedroom are a prime site for this. The damage is often viewed as some kind of mysterious fault of the building – ie. the house suffers from "damp", which can only be cured by the divine ministrations of a "specialist". As we approach the millennium, the prevalence of these medieval attitudes is worrying. You don't think so? For "damp" try saying "evil spirits", and for "specialist" insert "exorcist". Our late-20th century culture is full of witchcraft, and nowhere is it more prevalent than in the construction industry.

Why should this be? It doesn't help, of course, that in our

Western culture technology is thought of as inferior to the arts, to the extent that people who would be ashamed to admit to poor reading and writing skills actually like to boast about their innumeracy – "Oh, I'm useless with figures, ha ha". Whilst a lack of knowledge about films or paintings can be held up as a sign of ignorance, an inability to fix a dripping tap or change a fuse is hailed as an endearing eccentricity – proof that the owner's mind is on "higher" things. And yet, buildings are *important* in peoples' lives – we all spend most of our time in them. And when we go on holiday we visit them – museums, churches, castles. Past civilisations are defined by the remains of their buildings; in some cases, such as Stonehenge and the Peruvian pyramids, these may be *all* that remain.

Most importantly of all, buying a home remains the major financial transaction in most peoples' lives. And still the population at large remains fundamentally ignorant about how buildings are put together. Hang on, did I just say the population at large? For God's sake, half the people who describe themselves as property professionals don't know how buildings are put together. I mean Estate Agents, of course, but also many Surveyors and some Architects.

The building industry, like nature, abhors a vacuum. If there is a widespread gap in the public's knowledge, then this creates a market opportunity, and someone will always be crafty enough to come along and exploit it. You should make it your business to find out how your home works; because if you don't, someone else will surely turn up to fill the gap in your knowledge – very often with a bit of hocus-pocus.

Damp Behind the Ears (5/10/97)

Viewed from outer space, the Earth is a very wet planet; over 70% of its surface is covered with liquid water. Huge masses of ice cover the poles, and there are billions of tonnes of water vapour floating around in the atmosphere.

Not that I've ever been to outer space, of course, but I've seen the pictures and, whilst NASA might have removed the Stealth bombers on recce over Kamchatka, I can't really see them airbrushing out entire continents. The blue wavy stuff is for real, and there's loads of it. So much, in fact, that under normal conditions everything on Earth, including building materials, contains a bit of water: bricks, timber, plaster, wallpaper – even when they're dry they're wet, if you see what I mean. We call this the hygroscopic or "air dry" moisture content, and it can range from around 2% for old lime plaster up to 15% for pine floor boards. This is a perfectly natural state for building materials to be in; if they were any dryer they might crumble or crack.

The reason I mention all this is that there are companies with a vested interest in persuading the public that water is a bad thing, and that chemical methods are needed to keep it out of their homes. Of course, they don't refer to it as water, because water has a nice positive, thirst-quenching sound to it. Instead they call it damp, which sounds nasty and negative enough for you to want to get rid of it.

Now, the idea that water is bad and dryness is good is actually contrary to all biological sense; our bodies contain 65% water, and we are far more comfortable in moist conditions than dry ones – lost in a rain forest you could survive for months, but abandoned in the desert you'd be dead within hours. So how has moisture in buildings become so demonised? It has happened quite recently; the term "rising damp" was not coined until the 1960s, when it was first used in the marketing literature of the damp-proofing companies. Before that, if a house was standing on such wet ground that water was being sucked up by the brickwork, then draining the land was the usual remedy. It was only when silicone water repellents were developed that someone had the idea of squirting them into walls to form chemical damp-proof courses. To commercially exploit this idea it was necessary to convince the public that "rising damp" was a widespread and dangerous problem. This has been achieved very effectively; it's become like the old joke about sanity – I'm sane, and I've got a certificate to prove it.

I have been quoted recently in the building press as saying I don't think rising damp exists. I think it is a myth, like unicorns and fairies. The response from the damp-proofing industry has been swift and predictable; if rising damp doesn't exist, they fume, then why are there 2000 companies in existence whose sole purpose is to eradicate it? And why do councils and mortgage lenders ask for guarantees that it has been treated?

Well, it's the Emperor's new clothes, isn't it? You can't see the rising damp, and it has never given you any problems, but the specialist says he can detect it with his little meter, so you'll have to have it "treated".

This has given me a business idea. I'm going to spray peoples' homes with a delicately-scented colourless liquid, and issue paper guarantees that no unicorns will appear for another 25 years. At a monkey a piece – I should soon be able to retire.

Getting the Horn (23/11/97)

This week's column contains more than its share of smut, but I trust this will not be a problem for the liberal-minded readers of the Independent on Sunday. After all, the building game is fairly heaving with testosterone, and if you've got the builders in at home you'll know what I mean.

Smut hit me in the face, as it were, as I was musing over my proposed unicorn-proofing service. My idea, you may recall, is to spray houses with a colourless liquid, and issue 25 year guarantees against unicorn infestation. It seems to work for the rising damp boys, and apparently that's just as much of a myth.

Anyway, the most important factor in business success is

obviously choosing the right name, one that the punters are going to find easily in the Yellow Pages. Anything starting with Unicorn is going to come pretty low down in the alphabetical order; Aardvark is the name that's going to get you first in the list. Or so I thought until I checked in the phone book; to my surprise the Aardvarks and the Aarons don't get a look in until page nine. Because what come before that are letters, as in AA, A&A and AAA, and before that, numbers, starting with zero. So the first entry in the London "Business and Services" phone book is the 00000001A1 Agency which, in response to my call, were unable to offer anything in the plumbing, central heating or electrical line, not without a considerable stretch of the imagination, that is. In fact, the first twenty or so numbers all seem to be for firms offering what I believe are called personal services. It is not until half way down the page that you encounter the first plumber, called, with admirable restraint, 1A Action Plumbers. Whoever 1A Action Plumbers are, they deserve our support – they are in there at the cutting edge, and they are offering a service. I salute them; I will never criticise plumbers in this column again.

I should point out here, for the benefit of readers in the provinces, that the amount of number crunching you have to go through before you get to the first plumber can vary according to locality. In the Ipswich and District book, for example, the personal services industry does not seem to have got the hang of it; or maybe there is nothing of that sort going on up there. Whatever, 1st Call Pest Control are in pole position in Ipswich, and good luck to them – I shall be contacting them shortly with an offer of a lucrative unicorn-proofing franchise.

Smut item number two concerns that modern den of iniquity, the internet. Now, I am not in the habit of reading FHM magazine, but an interesting cutting from that journal has been sent to me by a young reader. It is an interview with Bob Guccione, founder of Penthouse. Mr Guccione discovered that "surfers" logging on to the Penthouse name, and expecting to be rewarded with pictures of naked women, were instead being directed to the web-site of a firm of roofers. The extraordinary coda to this incident is that Mr Guccione, instead of unleashing the full forces of the legal profession upon these enterprising scoundrels, actually gave them $10,000 to go away. I may be missing something here, but I can assure you, if I find anyone messing with my unicorn idea on the world-wide web, they won't be in line for a spray-off, er, I mean pay-off.

Woodworm – the Hole in the Argument (16/11/97)

I have come across an interesting passage in a decorating book called "Period Finishes and Effects". It reads, "Evidence of woodworm infestation can be effectively simulated by making clusters of small holes with a nail or the point of a compass". So now it becomes clear – half the population is trying to make new wood look old by poking holes in it, and the other half is spraying the holes with nasty chemicals in case something pokes its head out and bites them. You couldn't make it up.

As it happens, a friend called last week to ask what to do about his woodworm. He's a Building Surveyor by profession, so naturally he doesn't know anything about timber infestation. Like most people, he assumed the little holes in the edges of his floorboards were evidence of wood-boring insect attack. I told him that the holes may well be evidence that the boards once *had* woodworm, but since they are known in the trade as flight holes, what they actually indicate is that the insects have now scarpered. It is the larvae – the maggot stage – of *Anobium punctatum* that do the munching, and they do it below the surface of the timber. After a couple of years they pupate into little chrysalises, and then they hatch out as adult beetles, chomp their way to the surface and take off into the wild blue.

So why do surveyors think flight holes – or compass holes, as we shall now call them – are evidence of continuing insect attack? After all, active infestation is easy to confirm – the munching larvae produce faeces which consist largely, you will not be surprised to learn, of wood. It looks like sawdust, feels gritty when rubbed between the fingers, and can be collected on a sheet of paper under the suspect area.

I have made one or two observations about woodworm: first, *Anobium's* staple diet is sapwood – the outer, growing, part of the tree. They like the sapwood because it is moist and nutritious, so they hang out in places where there is plenty of fresh sapwood available – forests, for example. Now, while they are in the egg stage, they may suffer the indignity of being in a tree which is sawn up and carted off to be used as building timber. For as long as the timber retains enough moisture, they will carry on with their munching and burrowing, complete their normal life cycle and then buzz off, leaving flight holes. But by that time the timber will have dried down to an unpalatable level, especially if it is in a centrally-heated building, so there is little attraction for the female beetles to lay their eggs in the same spot; they'll be off outside looking for a nice fresh juicy tree. I suspect that most woodworm damage occurs in this fresh timber, probably in the first couple of years after the house is built; and since it is confined to the sapwood at the edges of boards and joists, there is rarely any structural weakening, and so no real problem.

Also, the term timber "infestation" is sometimes confused with "infection". It makes woodworm sound like some kind of contagious disease – I've known people who've bought old furniture at the auctions get paranoid that they've imported woodworm into their homes – they think the little blighters are going to spread out and eat the whole house, so they've sprayed chemicals everywhere. Left to themselves the woodworm will probably clear off – it's the long-term effects of the chemicals that are starting to look like the real problem.

Rat Race (7/12/98)

The test for the safety of timber treatment chemicals is known as the LD50. This may sound like something you spray on your bike chain, but it stands for Lethal Dose 50 per cent; that is, the amount of the chemical that will kill half the population. Chemicals affect different species in different ways, so the tests to find safe limits for people are carried out on other mammals, mainly rats. The LD50 is expressed in milligrams per kilogram of bodyweight (mg/kg), so if, for example, a one milligram dose is found to kill half the population of a group of rats with average body weight 200 grams, then the LD50 would be 5 mg/kg. This would put it in the deadly poison category, along with a substance like arsenic pentoxide (LD50 8mg/kg), commonly used to pre-treat building timbers.

Now, it is clear that if you use toxic chemicals in places where people come into contact with them, such as their homes, then there has to be some kind of testing, and measuring how much it takes to kill a fellow creature is certainly one method.

But what I have always wondered is, what about the other 50 per cent of the rats, the ones that didn't die? I mean, are they still happily running around in their little wheels, or are they starting to feel a bit off their food? And what about their mental state? You couldn't blame them for feeling a bit depressed, of course, what with half their mates dropping dead next to them, but can you tell whether their near-lethal dose has left them confused, nauseous, weak, or short of breath, the symptoms commonly reported by people who claim to have suffered pesticide poisoning? Of course not, not unless you interview them in rat language. So, understandably, there has not been much published about non-fatal exposure to timber treatments, and this has been a problem for the hundreds of people who have been affected by chemicals sprayed in their homes; for the LD50 is only a study of *acute* toxicity, not of the *chronic* effects of exposure to lower levels over a longer term. And remember, the timber treatment companies give 25 year guarantees, so they must reckon on the stuff staying active for that length of time.

So, people have had timber treatment chemicals sprayed in their homes and then felt ill, but their symptoms have been quite general – headaches, runny nose etc – and they may not have associated them with the treatment. If they have, then they will probably have felt better in a few days, and put it down to 'just one of those things'. If they felt like complaining, they probably wouldn't know who to complain to. For this reason it is thought that cases of pesticide poisoning are very largely under-reported. The chemical companies prefer to say that pesticide poisoning is very rare, because so few cases come to their attention.

Now, I don't know what the long-term effects of living in a house sprayed with pesticides are; I don't know because nobody knows. But I do keep thinking about that LD50 test; because it means that a baby weighing, say, four kilograms, will be affected by a dose of chemical *twenty times* more than an adult weighing 80 kilograms. And babies and children do tend to crawl around on the floorboards and put things in their mouths and all that. I really don't mean to be alarmist, and I don't want to scare parents; I just think it is time we did some proper research and found out the facts.

Move Over Lineus (18/1/98)

OK, hands up those who understood the Latin in last week's column. *Praestat sero quam nunquam* – "Better late than never". Don't worry if you didn't get it; I only know it myself because I used to have it on my letterhead. Latin's a dead language these days, only taught in public schools and seminaries. Which makes it all the more strange that the rag-bag of former plasterers and double-glazing salesmen who call themselves timber infestation surveyors are so fond of using it to describe the state of your floorboards. Woodworm, madam? – oh yes, that's *Anobium punctatum*, that is, very nasty. And the dry rot under the bath? – *Serpula lacrymans*, good job you called us in, sir, that'll spread all over the house, that will.

So these chancers, some of whom have problems stringing together three words in English, pepper their survey reports with Latin, as though they mis-spent their youth hanging around the natural history museum. They do it because it sounds as though they have made a thorough scientific diagnosis, and also because a Latin name sounds like a medical condition, and that justifies the drastic chemical cure they want to sell you.

Woodworm and dry rot are actually best dealt with by traditional building practices – fixing water leaks, providing good ventilation, and making sure the heating works. But most timber treatment "specialists" have only one aim, and that is to peddle chemicals.

Several readers have reported that their homes, having been sprayed with pesticides, are still infested with dry rot. This can only be because the original conditions which allowed the fungus to flourish – namely wet timbers and high humidity – are still present. If this is the case then chemical treatments are pointless; the moisture will eventually dilute them. And in any case, chemical sprays only coat the surface of the timber – I have seen dry rot growing through the centre of a damp, but treated, floor joist.

The name dry rot is unfortunate, as it gives the impression that the fungus grows without water, which is not so. True, it can spread some distance away from its starting point, and thus grow across dry sections of timber and even masonry, but it still needs water at its source – a great deal of water, in fact – so that dry rot is normally caused by leaking rainwater pipes or plumbing leaks. It also needs at least 75 per cent relative humidity – which can only occur where there is no ventilation. So dry rot thrives in enclosed spaces with water leaks – such as under baths and under timber ground floors. Remove the source of water and increase the ventilation and the fungus cannot survive; it's as simple as that. And if you take these measures then there is no need for poisonous chemicals.

It would be nice to be able to report that timber treatment firms which belong to the various trade associations offer a more objective service, but unfortunately this is not the case. In my experience they are all after only one thing – to sell chemicals. In fact the surveyors from the more "reputable" firms can often be the worst, because they are driven by performance targets as well as sales commissions – and, of course, they are sent on courses to learn the Latin names. Oh well, as Nero himself might have said, *Die dulci fruere*. ["Have a nice day" – ed.]

Birds and Bees (and Bats) (26/10/97)

Apparently, none of us is ever more than five metres away from a rat. Alright, stop sniggering at the back there, I am referring to *Rattus norvegicus*. Unfortunately, the same can no longer be said about many other creatures. Lots of the cute little furred and feathered things that used to live cheek by jowl with us are now, sadly, in steep decline. When did you last see a badger or a hare? Have you ever seen a woodpecker?

Modern intensive farming methods must take the lion's share of the blame, but the latest building techniques are also responsible for the decline of some species, since the loss of natural woodlands as breeding places meant that many animals and birds adapted by using buildings. But now, as our buildings become ever more sealed against the external environment, we are removing this option too.

Bats are a prime example of animals which have come to depend upon buildings for homes, hanging around in roofs by day and coming out at dusk, looking either cute or spooky, depending on your point of view. But bats also perform a valuable function around houses, because they feed on insects – up to 3000 a day – and so help to keep insect numbers down. Unfortunately, the current practices of sealing eaves with bat-proof and bird-proof ventilation grilles, and filling cavity walls with insulation, mean that bats have far fewer roosting sites, and so are experiencing a rapid decrease in numbers. The recent practice of spraying timber treatment chemicals in loft spaces has also taken its toll on the bat population. The Wildlife and Countryside Act of 1981 achieved a notable success in protecting bats, especially against organo-chlorine insecticides, so that it is now actually a criminal offence to kill or injure bats by spraying roof spaces in which they are living. Cynics have noted that it is still not an offence to harm human beings by spraying unnecessary chemicals in their homes, but that's another story.

Swifts are another creature whose exclusion from our buildings is causing a rapid decline in numbers. As their natural cave and cliff nest sites are rare in Britain, swifts that migrate here from Africa have survived by nesting in buildings. When the birds leave the nest they need a clear drop of at least five metres to gather speed and become airborne, so gaps in eaves and gables make ideal sites. Older buildings used to provide plenty of such nesting places, but modern ones are effectively swift-proof. Again, this is to our disadvantage, as adult swifts catch around 600 insects per hour to feed their chicks, and so are an excellent natural control of insect life around buildings.

What is unfortunate about all of this is that we have known for years that we are pushing other species into extinction, and yet we seem to be incapable of altering our behaviour. Very minor measures in new buildings would provide suitable nesting and roosting sites, without the bother of putting up and maintaining nesting boxes. Very small gaps in eaves soffit ventilation grilles – 35 x 65 mm – will provide nest holes for swifts, whilst being too small for pigeons or starlings. Bats, which are completely harmless, can be encouraged to roost in special "bat bricks" in gables and in ventilated ridge tiles, without allowing them access into the loft space itself. This not just sentimentality, but in our own best interests – we should encourage these flying insect catchers do us all a favour.

Further information from: The Bat Conservation Trust, 0171-627 2629; Concern for Swifts, 01760 756466.

Measuring Up (6/7/97)

Most British people seem to be baffled by the metric system. It is supposed to have been taught in schools for at least 20 years, but few people seem to be able to tell you their height in metres or their weight in kilograms. Apart from builders, that is. The British building industry went metric in 1970. In fact, it went rather more metric than might have been wise – instead of metres and centimetres, the unit of linear measurement adopted was the millimetre. Now, measuring in millimetres is eminently sensible if you want to avoid ambiguity – you can measure anything from the thickness of an electric cable up to the height of a house using the same units; no commas, no decimal points. You don't even have to write "mm" after the figure – since the whole industry is supposed to be using the same system, there is only one thing your dimension can mean. So town houses are around 5000 wide, door openings are 2100 high, sheets of plasterboard are 1200 by 2400, and each course of bricks measures 75. Brilliant. There's just one catch. The great British public still uses the imperial system.

Now, quite why British school children are still only able to tell you their heights in feet and inches, and their weights in stones and pounds, is unclear. My guess is that, owing to the indifference of the wider public, children learn to associate the metric system with maths and science at school, but are unable to relate it to the world around them. This is hardly surprising when Estate Agents and mortgage valuation Surveyors – for most people the only building professionals they ever encounter – insist on using imperial measurement. No doubt they would counter with the argument that feet and inches are what people understand. But how are people ever going to understand the metric system if they never have to use it?

For example, there was a predictable outcry in the media last year when food weights in supermarkets were finally made to go

111

metric. A succession of bewildered old dears was dragged in front of the cameras and quizzed on conversion factors from pounds to kilograms. For supermarket shopping the conversion factor is an irrelevance, of course – you either use pounds or you use kilos. You pick up a lump of cheese that looks about the right size and then you look to see how much it costs. Making a story out of the innumeracy of old age pensioners takes attention away from the real issue surrounding mensuration, which is that, under the last government, weights and measures inspections by Trading Standards Officers were pared down to a bare minimum, and cheating by retailers has become, consequently, commonplace. If ever you need petrol for your lawnmower, take an empty 5 litre can along and see how much the pump reads after you've filled it up to the line – you'll see what I mean.

The other issue, that the British building industry uses millimetres while our continental cousins use centimetres, shouldn't really make a difference, but it does. Most tape measures are calibrated in centimetres, and it is easy to forget to multiply by the factor of ten, so 3 m 40 cm can get written down as 3040 rather than 3400. Errors like this can leave an embarrassingly big gap in your new kitchen work top.

Fitted kitchens, by the way, often exhibit distinctive symptoms of mis-measurement. They are called wine racks. A wine rack under the work top usually indicates a cock-up, or at least idleness, in the chippy's calculations. Two wine racks are a sign of measurement meltdown.

Skip (1/6/97)

You know you're getting old when you stop taking things out of skips and start dumping stuff in them. The best site for a skip, then, would appear to be in an area with a good mix of ages, where it can act as a recycling centre. The other morning I arrived on site to find a standard lamp on top of the pile. By ten o'clock it had gone. If only I'd put a £5 price sticker on it, to reward me for supplying the premises for the exchange.

For the builder, of course, arriving at work to find that your expensive skip space has been taken up by a mattress or wardrobe can be a major pain. The problem is endemic in cities, where the skip has to be left in the street – the neighbours can see it as a chance to clear out the shed, or an incentive to finally get rid of that old three-piece suite.

Other cases of skip abuse are more subtle. Secret drinkers often dump their empties in skips, for fear, I suppose, of what the dustmen might think. On one job, every morning would reveal another empty brandy bottle neatly wrapped in newspaper (the *Daily Telegraph*, in case you're wondering) and slipped under the tarpaulin cover. A skip on another site harvested a steady supply of porno mags, to great delight all round; that was the only job I've ever known where the plumber turned up every morning. There was one specialist publication devoted to practices involving funnels and lengths of rubber tubing, however, which even the plumber wasn't keen on.

Some builders have found worse things; murder weapons are routinely tossed into skips; and a few years ago a dismembered body was found distributed in several skips around north London.

But bottles, magazines and even arms and legs don't take up too much space. It's the wardrobes and carpets, and sacks of garden rubbish, that cost the builder dear, especially since the landfill tax raised the average cost of skip hire to around £125.

Some builders get obsessive about skip abuse, rifling through the bin bags and cardboard boxes for evidence of ownership. This usually shows up, on envelopes or in diaries, and the offending refuse is then triumphantly tipped in front of the perpetrator's house. Some interesting confrontations can ensue, a recurring theme being that people think skips are provided for the public good; "the council pays for it" is often offered in mitigation, despite the slogan 'McGrath Bros', or 'Supaskips' emblazoned on the side.

So what's to be done? A tarpaulin stretched across the top can help give the impression the skip is full, and discourage the wardrobe-and-mattress crowd. But some people will just toss stuff onto the tarpaulin – sometimes the first job on a Monday is to retrieve the tarpaulin from under a hundred Kentucky Fried Chicken cartons, or a wardrobe. Or the tarpaulin may get nicked. You can hire covered skips, but these work out pricey. In the end, most builders learn to take the rough with the smooth; you do get some useful stuff dumped in your skip; years ago I found a box of artist's materials, which has kept me in small brushes and 4H pencils to this day. One labourer I had used to rummage through the bags of clothes for shirts and trousers to use for work.

But listen, if you want to get rid of stuff, don't expect some poor builder to pay for it. Just put it in front of the house with a sign saying, free to good home. Together we can end this skip abuse.

INDEX

Architects 30, 37, 54, 77, 80, 84, 85, 92, 98

Ball valve 17
Bricklaying 9, 20, 31, 48
Brickwork 10, 26, 36
Builders 16, 47, 52, 54, 80, 89, 97, 113
Builders' merchants 9, 10, 15
Building Engineer 19

Carpets 7, 8, 13
Cavity walls 28, 30, 31, 109
Cement 9, 10, 54, 92, 93
Central heating 19, 64, 94, 101, 104
Chemicals 12, 19, 104
Chipboard 13
Cistern 17, 63, 66
Concrete 20, 22, 40
Condensation 18, 19, 26, 27, 94, 97
Cracks 10, 26, 34, 37, 38

DIY 7, 9, 14, 15
Dampness 33, 54, 78, 97, 99
Damp-proofing 13, 80, 99, 100
Decorating 7, 12
Double glazing 19, 25, 54, 82
Draught proofing 19
Drink 69, 70, 72, 113
Dry rot 106, 107

Electrics 7, 10, 101

Fireplaces 40, 41
Foundations 37, 51
Floor boards 16, 41, 106
Fungicides 12, 13

Garden walls 20
Gutters 14, 15, 18, 22, 32

Hardcore 20
Hardboard 7

Insulation 13, 31

Lime 9, 21, 22, 39, 89, 90, 92, 93

MDF 13, 37
Maintenance 14, 15, 21, 28
Mortar 9, 10, 93

Paint 13, 18, 23, 53
Paving 20
Plasterboard 13, 89
Plastering 7, 89, 91
Plasticiser 9
Plumbing 10, 16, 60, 62, 101
Pointing 92

Rising damp 57, 99, 100
Roofs, roofing 10, 16, 17, 27, 84